The Banana Split Book

Everything There Is To Know
About America's Greatest Dessert

Michael Turback

Camino Books, Inc.

Philadelphia

Manufactured in the United States of America

1 2 3 4 5 07 06 05 04

Library of Congress Cataloging-in-Publication Data

Turback, Michael.
   The banana split book : everything there is to know about America's
greatest dessert / Michael Turback.
      p. cm.
   ISBN 0-940159-83-X
   1. Banana splits. I. Title.

   TX795.T75 2004
   641.8'62—dc22   2004001389

Cover and interior design: Jerilyn Bockorick

All Chiquita-related materials are used with permission from Chiquita
Brands International, Inc.

This book is available at a special discount on bulk purchases for
promotional, business, and educational use.

Publisher
Camino Books, Inc.
P. O. Box 59026
Philadelphia, PA 19102

www.caminobooks.com

Contents

Acknowledgments

Writing a book on the topic of the Banana Split has been an eminently agreeable task, aided and abetted by many people who gave so generously of their time and expertise:

My thanks to Carl Mattioli, president of the Latrobe Historical Society, who offered a dutiful recounting of local history. To the families of David Strickler and E. R. "Brady" Hazard, who searched their memories for recollections and their attics for photographs. To Joe Greubel, Don Orlando, Pam Villagran, David Lebovitz, Joe Calderone, Barbara Lang, Etienne Merle, Ray Klavon, Tom Levkulic, Debbie Stamper, J. B. Stamper, Judy Gano, Kay Fisher, Mary Gibson, Pat Larrick, Laura Frankel, Jim Powers, Pete Murphy, Steve Glickbarg, Tim Mathias, Dennis Cronin, Barb Wurtz, Aubrey Zinaich, Eric Lackey, Jerry Smith, Niall Bowen, Cedric Yapp, Don Oshop, Richard Warnock, Chris Calloway, Trevor White, Brian Mahoney, Brian Mack, Rosy Bergin, Melissa Johnson, Ray Borkman, Ray Peck, Patrick McCurdy, Ken Martin, Jason McConnell, Wendy Lund, Ken Bannister, Ann Lovell, Todd Bolton, Chip Hawkins, Rick Bayless, Eric Bromberg, Gary Theodore, Tim Love, Mark Arriola, James Foran, Elizabeth Faulkner, Bill Smart, Jeffrey Turback, Lynn Bolton, and Mike Mitchell (for the good folks at Chiquita Brands International). I daresay this book could not have been possible without them.

My deepest appreciation to Cornell Hotel School students Kate Hawley and Kathryn Parkin for their boundless energy and brilliant research.

Thanks to all the soda fountains, restaurants, and belly boutiques that keep the Banana Split tradition alive and well, to the many chefs and fountaineers who have graciously shared their views and their recipes, and especially to Norman Van Aken, restaurateur extraordinaire.

To editors Michelle Scolnick and Barbara Gibbons and designer Jerilyn Bockorick—thanks for the hard work.

To my editor and publisher, Edward Jutkowitz of Camino Books, for his enthusiastic support of this project and his unswerving belief in its success.

Special thanks to my wife, Juliet, an integral part of my writing career, for offering staunch support and encouragement whenever needed. Together we have traveled halfway around the world, sharing wonderful experiences and countless Banana Splits.

And, finally, I want to acknowledge the most important people in the life of this book—the readers. Thank you!

Introduction

Americans like a good story—especially about themselves. While *The Banana Split Book* is obviously about the concoction of bananas and ice cream, it is also a revealing portrait of America.

The banana is a nutritious source of fiber and potassium in our diets, a comic prop that has induced giggles and snorts since Charlie Chaplin started slipping on its peels, and an object of sexual innuendo ever since Mae West wondered if her boyfriend had one in his pocket.

The proof, of course, is in the tasting, and at its peak of ripeness the banana's soft, pillowy texture and sweet, brilliant fruit flavor are oh-so-easy to love. That's probably why each and every one of us consumes 29 pounds of those little yellow boomerangs every year. But sooner or later our bananas meet up with ice cream, and whenever they do, it's magic time!

Assembling a Banana Split is a primal culinary exercise and an opportunity for spectacle. Eating one unleashes 10 different ingredients, fighting each other for your attention. It is at once highbrow, lowbrow, flashy and trashy, foolish, fancy, and unapologetically eccentric. It is much more, of course, than the sum of its parts, and, not surprisingly, every August 25 is set aside to celebrate National Banana Split Day and to preserve the dessert's precious place in our nation's culture.

More than any other native dish, the Banana Split is an essential vintage reminder of the American genius for invention, passion for indulgence, and reputation for wackiness. It's like no other dessert in the world—a grand idea that could only have been conceived in a place as grand as America.

Michael Turback

The Banana Split Book

Chapter 1

Curiosity of the Indies

❝ While forbidden fruit is said to taste sweeter, it usually spoils faster. ❞

— Abigail Van Buren

What can you say about the world's most common fruit? Well, a lot, actually. The banana has been cultivated and consumed since ancient times, even predating the cultivation of rice. According to Hindu and Muslim teachings, the banana— not the apple—was the culinary temptation in the Garden of Eden, and banana leaves—not fig leaves—provided outfits for Adam and Eve. The banana plant is, apparently, an original inhabitant of India.

In his march across Asia, Alexander the Great took every opportunity to learn about local customs and to taste native foods in the places he vanquished. Reaching the valley of the river Indus in 327 B.C., Alexander encountered sages who meditated under the shady, green leaves of banana plants, and whose diets consisted entirely of bananas. He was convinced that their wisdom came from eating the banana, and he called it "fruit of the wise men."

Alexander the Great

The Cure for What Ails You

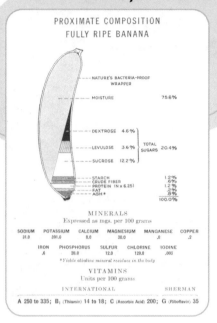

PROXIMATE COMPOSITION
FULLY RIPE BANANA

NATURE'S BACTERIA-PROOF WRAPPER

MOISTURE 75.6%

DEXTROSE   4.6%
LEVULOSE   3.6%   } TOTAL SUGARS 20.4%
SUCROSE   12.2%

STARCH 1.2%
CRUDE FIBER 6%
PROTEIN (N x 6.25) . 1.2%
FAT 2%
ASH * 8%
                   100.0%

MINERALS
Expressed as mgs. per 100 grams

SODIUM	POTASSIUM	CALCIUM	MAGNESIUM	MANGANESE	COPPER
31.0	391.0	8.0	30.0	.8	.2

IRON	PHOSPHORUS	SULFUR	CHLORINE	IODINE
.6	28.0	12.0	129.0	.003

*Yields alkaline mineral residues in the body

VITAMINS
Units per 100 grams

INTERNATIONAL   SHERMAN

A 250 to 335; B₁ (Thiamin) 14 to 18; C (Ascorbic Acid) 200; G (Riboflavin) 35

If you suffer from hemorrhoids, you might heed the advice of an old folk remedy and apply a banana peel to your painful posterior. Bananas contain a sugar that can be applied to topical infections because it has mild antimicrobial properties.

People who enjoy snow sports may experience mild episodes of frostbite if they are exposed to the cold for too long. Applying the inside of the banana skin to the frostbitten area will bring immediate relief.

Bananas absorb excess stomach acid and relieve pain from ulcers.

American folklore gives credit to the banana for helping to lower blood pressure, relieve constipation, and cure corns, warts, and even stage fright.

Side-Splitting

Standard props of silent film comedies included buckets and mops, ladders, fences, revolving doors, electric fans, Limburger cheese, pies, and, of course, banana peels.

Playwright Charles MacArthur was brought to Hollywood to produce a screenplay for Charlie Chaplin, but was finding it difficult to write visual jokes for the comic legend.

"What's the problem?" asked Chaplin.

"How, for example, could I make a fat lady, walking down Fifth Avenue, slip on a banana peel and still get a laugh? It's been done a million times," said MacArthur. "What's the best way to *get* the laugh? Do I show the banana peel first, then the fat lady approaching, then she slips? Or do I show the fat lady first, then the banana peel, and *then* she slips?"

"Neither," said Chaplin without a moment's hesitation. "You show the fat lady approaching. Then you show the banana peel; then you show the fat lady and the banana peel together; then she steps *over* the banana peel and disappears down a manhole."

India has always intrigued and fascinated the rest of the world, and explorers ultimately helped bananas reach Egypt, Africa, and the Canary Islands. In 1516, a Spanish missionary named Friar Tomas de Berlanga carried a bit of the exotic to the New World when he transported the first banana root stocks across the Atlantic from the Canaries and planted them in the rich alluvial Caribbean soil, where they thrived.

Historian Gonzalo Fernandez de Oviedo y Valdes wrote, "A special kind of fruit was brought to this city of Santo Domingo, whence they [*sic*] spread to the other settlements of this Island and to all other islands peopled by Christians. And they were even carried to the mainland, and in every port they flourished. . . ."

In 1870, schooner master Lorenzo Dow Baker from Wellfleet, on Cape Cod, bought 1,400 stems of bananas in Port Antonio, Jamaica, and sold them two weeks later in Jersey City, New Jersey, at a considerable profit. Returning to Jamaica, he visited coastal farms, where he urged

Captain Lorenzo Dow Baker, the first banana merchant.

❝ The first man who has ten acres of bananas will be rich! ❞

— Captain Lorenzo Baker, encouraging Jamaicans to plant bananas

Moving Up in the World

In 1936, the first ski resort in the United States, Sun Valley, used a chairlift that was based on a hoist used for hauling bananas into a ship's hold.

Nothing to Sneeze At

Individuals who are sensitive to ragweed (*Ambrosia*) pollen may experience symptoms when eating a banana.

Bananabilia

In addition to high humidity and sweltering heat, bananas need loose soil with high organic content to grow. Bananas are mature about three months from the time of flowering, with each bunch producing about 10 "hands," or rows, of about 20 bananas each. A bunch will yield about 200 "fingers," or bananas. An average bunch of bananas can weigh between 80 and 125 pounds. Two-man teams harvest the bananas. While one man whacks the bunch with his machete, another catches the falling bunch on his shoulders.

" A stockbroker urged me to buy a stock that would triple its value every year. I told him, 'At my age, I don't even buy green bananas. "

— Claude D. Pepper (D-FL), who served
in Congress to the age of 88

" The adjective is the banana peel of the parts of speech. "

— Clifton Paul Fadiman

Heading My Way?

It was a common sight in Captain Lorenzo Baker's Jamaica to see a group of a dozen or more peasant farm women called higglers, each with a large bunch of bananas on her head, sometimes traveling for several miles without stopping. They were taught from childhood to carry everything on their heads. Schoolchildren played tag with books, and even ink bottles, on their heads. When a Jamaican belle went to a social function she carried her shoes on her head, and she put them on her feet when she reached her destination. Everything from a postage stamp to a Saratoga trunk was transported in this way.

the islanders to grow more bananas. It was still a local crop, grown and reaped for local markets, but Captain Baker was certain of a more lucrative market in the United States. Baker himself confessed a personal liking for what he called "the dadblamed silly fruit."

In his book, *Empire in Green and Gold*, Charles Morrow Wilson recounts how Baker slowly and steadily built the banana trade: "With good seamanship and stowage, Jamaica bananas, cut green and thin, were carried to the port of Boston in fourteen to seventeen days of sailing time . . . . then assisted by several dozen determined peddlers who were waiting with their baskets and handcarts."

During the centennial year of 1876, Philadelphia was host to a celebration of 100 years of American cultural and industrial progress. The Centennial Exhibition attracted nearly 9 million citizens at a time when the population of the entire United States was only 46 million. Of the scores of new products on display, two attracted the most attention:

Table Manners

The "proper" way to eat a banana, according to *Debrett's Guide to Etiquette and Modern Manners*, is with a knife and fork: "The eating of fruit can be a social minefield for the uninitiated. Bananas must never be eaten monkey-style at the table. Firstly, peel with a knife, pulling off the skin in vertical strips. Cut off around one third of an inch at each end and then cut small discs of fruit and eat either with the fingers or a fork, if provided."

Show Me the Money

"Banana Day" was any day a ship was loading in Jamaica. Planters who had just sold produce for export celebrated by lighting their cigars with five-dollar bills.

Banana Bully

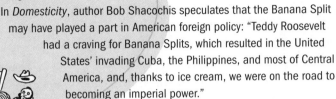

In *Domesticity*, author Bob Shacochis speculates that the Banana Split may have played a part in American foreign policy: "Teddy Roosevelt had a craving for Banana Splits, which resulted in the United States' invading Cuba, the Philippines, and most of Central America, and, thanks to ice cream, we were on the road to becoming an imperial power."

" The older you get, the better you get—unless you're a banana. "

— Henny Youngman

" When you are driving, where do you put your banana? "

— Honda HR-V sales brochure

Playground of the Rich and Famous

"The most exquisite port on earth" was the way American poet Ella Wheeler Wilcox described Port Antonio, Jamaica. In the 1940s and 1950s, Port Antonio provided the setting for numerous Hollywood films and was a favorite destination of many celebrities, including Clara Bow, William Randolph Hearst, Rudyard Kipling, Bette Davis, Ginger Rogers, and Errol Flynn. Flynn gushed that he "never met a woman as beautiful as Port Antonio," and he owned several properties there. Robin Moore, author of *The French Connection*, is said to have written the famous novel while sitting under a banana tree in Port Antonio.

an invention by Alexander Graham Bell that transmitted a speaker's voice to a listener's ear, and a yellow, crescent-shaped tropical fruit advertised as the "Curiosity of the Indies." Each banana was wrapped in foil and sold for 10 cents.

Other entrepreneurs quickly learned what Captain Baker had suspected all along: there was some serious money to be made from importing the fruit from lands where it grew in abundance. They formed companies, established banana plantations, developed means of transport, and promoted the consumption of bananas at every meal. By the beginning of the 20th century, the lust for profits had led to such a powerful network of railroads, steamships, and land acquisitions throughout Central America and the Caribbean region that American companies were able to exert extraordinary influence on the governments of the banana-producing countries. So entwined were these nations with the banana trade that the term *banana republic* was coined to describe them.

Spoils of War

After his defeat at Waterloo in 1815, Napoleon Bonaparte was exiled to the island of St. Helena in the South Atlantic, where exotic flora introduced from all parts of the world made the island a veritable botanical garden. Bananas, probably brought from Africa, grew freely. Napoleon remained there for the rest of his life, regularly feasting on banana fritters drenched in honey.

Dear Ann Landers

Advice columnist Ann Landers advised headache sufferers to apply the inside of one half of a banana peel to the forehead and the other half to the back of the neck. She noted that 85 percent of those who tried this cure found relief within 30 minutes.

Feed the World

Small farmers in developing countries produce 87 percent of the world's bananas, nearly all of which are grown and consumed locally. Half a billion people in Africa and Asia depend on bananas as a staple food. In some parts of the world, the word for banana is also the word for food.

" I went bananas. "

— Liza Minelli, explaining why she moved into the sheltered, regimented Barbizon Hotel for Women

" The most delicious thing in the world is a banana. "

— Benjamin Disraeli

Key Words

Banana Tree
showing Bud and Fruit
in Florida

Cavendish. The most common variety of bananas found in markets and grocery stores around the world, and the one that Americans consume to the tune of 29 pounds per person each year; a product of extensive hybridization both in nature and through human manipulation.

From our privileged position in the future, we now clearly see abuses in the business practices of banana cartels. While dictatorships and corruption existed in Central America long before the advent of the banana trade, the fruit companies exploited that corruption for their own benefit.

In 1907, President Theodore Roosevelt had a fleet of war-ships painted white and sent on a cruise to impress the world with America's sea power. The ships became known as the Great White Fleet. At about the same time, the United Fruit Company, the largest of the banana companies, had its own

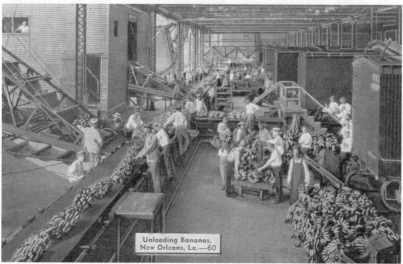

Unloading Bananas,
New Orleans, La.—60

ships painted white, but for more practical reasons. White reflected the tropical sun and allowed temperatures on board to be more easily maintained. As the fleet of commercial refrigerated vessels grew, it too became known as the Great White Fleet. Once cargoes arrived in ports, riverboats and transcontinental trains carried the fruit to cities throughout the United States, so a new market of consumers could enjoy bananas.

Bananas are long and curved, prepackaged by nature, with a firm, creamy flesh gift-wrapped inside a thick, inedible peel. Nothing beats the pleasure of savoring a fresh, just-ripe banana. It needs no washing, no preparation, and no special equipment. You just peel and eat.

We have also learned to enjoy the banana in combination with other favorite foods. Poet Walt Whitman dipped his bananas in sherry. President Calvin Coolidge covered his bananas with orange marmalade. Elvis Presley frequently munched on fried peanut-butter-and-banana sandwiches. And, since the mid-1920s, banana in cold cereal, corn flakes in particular, has proved the breakfast of choice for many Americans. But for the past 100 years, the concoction we call

Silent Cal

President Calvin Coolidge was known as a man of few words. On a visit to the gardens of the du Pont family in Delaware, he spent an hour in the great greenhouses, rich with a thousand varieties of exotic growths. He walked in silence until the end of the tour, when the party reached a room with familiar fruit-bearing tropical plants. The president stopped short, looked with evident interest, and spoke for the first and only time that afternoon. "Bananas," he said.

Calvin Coolidge, bananas at the White House.

the Banana Split has been, if not America's most popular dessert, then surely the most visible culinary symbol of our national indulgence.

The Banana Split has been tested by time. It is part of the history of a banana-eating nation, and if food preparation is an art, as we like to think it is, then our Banana Split is an American masterpiece—nothing less than that.

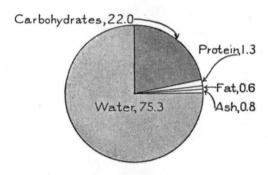

COMPOSITION

Three-fourths of the edible part of the banana is water.

Chiquita's **Fascinating Facts** ABOUT BANANA

AN EARLY SETTLE

BANANAS WERE INTRODUCED TO THE NEW WORLD BY SPANISH MISSIONARIES NOT LONG AFTER COLUMBUS. TODAY, CENTRAL AMERICA IS THE LARGEST PRODUCING AREA IN THE WORLD

BANANA "CITY"

BANANA-PRODUCING AREA IS
LARGE, WITH SO MANY PEOPLE
ORKING ON IT, THAT IT
ESEMBLES A SMALL TOWN, WITH
CHOOLS, HOSPITALS, STORES, ETC.

NATURE'S DUSTPROOF PACKAGE!

THE BANANA'S PEEL SE
IN AND PROTECTS ITS
GOODNESS UNTIL YOU'R
READY TO PEEL AND EAT
SO CONVENIENT, TOO!

FREE BOOK!
"HOW TO BE TOPS IN YOUR TEENS"

It's easy to be popular! This big, illustrated booklet is full of down-to-earth facts on grooming, personality, sports . . . fresh, smart tips on how to stand out as a leader in your crowd . . . do's and don'ts for both boys and girls. Fill in the coupon and send for your free copy today!

Chapter 2

The Pixilated Mr. Strickler

Man's mind, once stretched by a new idea, never regains its original dimensions.

— Oliver Wendell Holmes

Americans were starved for more exciting things to eat when the ice cream sundae arrived to save the day. In 1892, a soda jerk from Ithaca, New York, poured cherry syrup over a plain scoop of vanilla ice cream, then placed a candied cherry at the top. His customer was the local Unitarian minister, who insisted on naming the new dish after the day it was invented. When you find something you love, your first instinct is to tell anyone who will listen all about it and what makes it so wonderful. Cornell University students who frequented Chester Platt's soda fountain carried the recipe home with them on summer vacations, and there was no stopping history. By the beginning of the 20th century, "sundaes" had become part of American culture.

David E. Strickler was born on July 12, 1881, in Latrobe, a small town at the foothills of Pennsylvania's Allegheny Mountains. He was an ambitious, churchgoing young man

Happenstance

who, at the age of 16, obtained a position at the Tassell Pharmacy, where he served the apprenticeship necessary for a practical knowledge of pharmacology. Owner Dan Livengood stocked the store at 805 Ligonier Street with drugs and remedies prescribed by the medical profession, a complete line of proprietary tonics and salves, and fancy articles one would expect to find in an apothecary that dated back to the Civil War era.

In connection with his drug store, Livengood had a well-equipped oculist's department on the second floor, with facilities for testing the eyesight of his customers and fitting them with corrective spectacles. And in his establishment stood an A.D. Puffer soda fountain and ice cream well, where phosphates, sodas, and sundaes were made by affable clerks who were always ready to wait on patrons who filled the booths at the rear of the store.

Strickler was a destiny's child, who concocted ice cream sundaes and transformed them into something grander. During the summer of 1904 his dalliance with the tropical banana, sliced down the middle for easier eating, gave way to a flabbergasting fountain creation. Juxtaposing three scoops of different flavors of ice cream on the banana halves, he added three dollops of fruit syrups, combining three mini-sundaes into one. The effect was startling.

> **It's time for me to make like a banana and split.**
>
> — Milton Berle

Split Ends

Bananas are properly peeled from the non-stem end. This leaves most of the "strings" attached to the skin, obviating the need to remove them separately, and this method allows the stem end to be used as a handle.

Classic Banana Split

Split 1 banana lengthwise and place the halves parallel on a Banana Split dish. Place 1 scoop of vanilla ice cream between the banana halves. To the left of the vanilla place 1 scoop of chocolate ice cream, and to the right place 1 scoop of strawberry ice cream. Ladle 2 ounces of crushed pineapple over the vanilla, 2 ounces of chocolate syrup over the chocolate, and 2 ounces of strawberry topping over the strawberry ice cream. Garnish between the scoops of ice cream with whipped cream. Sprinkle with chopped mixed nuts, and place 2 whole cherries at the top.

Holiday Banana Split

Split 1 banana lengthwise and place the halves parallel on a Banana Split dish. Place 1 scoop of vanilla ice cream between the banana halves. On either side of the vanilla place 1 scoop of strawberry ice cream. Cover the vanilla ice cream with 2 tablespoons of chopped maraschino cherries, and cover the strawberry ice cream with 2 tablespoons of blueberries. Garnish with whipped cream, and sprinkle with chopped mixed nuts.

Hot Fudge Banana Split

Split 1 banana lengthwise and place slices parallel on a Banana Split dish. In between the banana halves place 1 scoop of chocolate ice cream. On either side place scoops of vanilla ice cream. Ladle 2 ounces of hot fudge over the ice cream, garnish with whipped cream, and place 5 or 6 salted almonds at the top.

With an eye for detail, Strickler even devised a way to display the main ingredient. After being sliced from stem to stern, the banana was skillfully placed in the glass dish so its inside cut was visible to the customer. Strickler was convinced this presentation would stimulate the appetite.

The steep price of 10 cents— double the cost of an ordinary sundae— did not prevent the students from nearby St. Vincent College from beating a path to his "Banana Split Sundae."

Across town, even rival Anderson's Drug Store was deluged with orders for the new dessert, and it wasn't long before this midsummer night's dream would engage the outside world. All Strickler needed to complete his masterwork was a dish that was shaped to be more functional, so he persuaded

> **" To have elegance, you have to make wine like a Banana Split: a touch of caramel, a touch of cream. "**
>
> — Matias Lecaros, winemaker at Chile's Carmen Winery

Locals Say "Lay-trobe"

Curiously, the Banana Split is not Latrobe's only claim to fame. This out-of-the-ordinary town is the lifelong residence of golfing great Arnold Palmer and the first "Neighborhood" of legendary children's TV-show host, Mr. Rogers. The first professional football game was played here in 1895, and the first air-mail pickup originated at the local airport in 1939. Latrobe has a monastery (St. Vincent), a brewery (Rolling Rock), and a professional football team (the Pittsburgh Steelers training camp). In 1997 Pennsylvania's House of Representatives passed Resolution No. 44, urging David Letterman's *Late Show* to name Latrobe as its "Home Office."

Melba Banana Split

Split 1 banana lengthwise and place the halves parallel on a Banana Split dish. Place 1 scoop of chocolate ice cream between the banana halves. To the left of the chocolate place 1 scoop of vanilla ice cream, and to the right place 1 scoop of peach ice cream. Arrange slices of a whole peach around the scoops of ice cream and ladle 2 ounces of melba sauce over all. Garnish between the scoops of ice cream with whipped cream, sprinkle with chopped mixed nuts, and top each whipped cream peak with a whole cherry.

School Days Banana Split

Split 1 banana lengthwise and place the halves parallel on a Banana Split dish. Place 2 scoops of vanilla ice cream between the banana halves. Ladle 1 ounce of hot fudge over all. Sprinkle with chopped mixed nuts, garnish between the scoops of ice cream with small rosettes of whipped cream, and place a whole cherry at the top.

Banana Boat

Split 1 banana lengthwise and place the halves parallel on a Banana Split dish. Place 1 scoop each of vanilla and chocolate ice cream between the banana halves. Ladle 2 ounces of chocolate syrup over all. Garnish with whipped cream, and add waffle cookies (pizzelles) for the boat's "sails."

Divided We Stand

A mystique, partly cultivated and partly spontaneous, has built up through the century regarding the correct procedure for assembling a Banana Split. Most Splits call for placement of the banana first, followed by the remaining ingredients. However, if the banana is added last, the toppings can slide down and around the sides of the ice cream, rather than over the sides of the dish.

the Westmoreland Glass Company in nearby Grapeville to press the world's first banana boats. These glass dishes were soon included in the company's product line, and sold for $1.50 a dozen. Sales grew, and so did the hyperbole.

Strickler himself always insisted that Dr. Howard Dovey was the person who was actually responsible for popularizing the Banana Split. After a stint as a clerk at Tassell Pharmacy, Dovey left Latrobe to attend medical school in Philadelphia, where he told fellow students what the folks back home were eating. He showed them how his friend Strickler assembled each ingredient in the long, narrow dish made expressly for the new dessert. The students, in turn, encouraged soda jerks in Philadelphia who enthusiastically embraced the notion, and, by the following summer, Banana Splits were being dished up on the boardwalk of Atlantic City, New Jersey—a gateway to the rest of the world. Success in the populous resort ensured immediate acceptance and widespread demand.

Tricks of the Trade

BANANA
ROYAL 1.75

BANANA 1.25
SPLIT
SPECIALTY OF THE HOUSE

The time-honored schematic for Banana Split construction starts with a fully ripe banana that has been split lengthwise with the peel on. Remove the peel, brush the halves with lemon juice (to keep the color bright), and place one half on either side of a clean, sparkling Banana Split dish. Working quickly, place three scoops of different flavors of ice cream in a row between the banana halves. Cover each scoop with a different topping, choosing syrups that complement the flavors of the ice cream. Then, for good measure, flood the dish with all three sauces. Garnish with lightly sweetened whipped cream (use it judiciously—you don't want to cover up too much of the effect of the toppings over the ice cream). Sprinkle crushed nuts lightly over the whipped cream, then place a whole cherry at the top. Serve immediately with a sundae spoon, a glass of ice water, and a napkin.

Merry-Go-Round Banana Split

*L*adle 2 ounces of cherry syrup into the bottom of an ice cream bowl. Add 1 scoop of vanilla ice cream (cone-shaped, if possible). Split 1 banana lengthwise, then cut the split halves again widthwise. Arrange the banana quarters vertically against the sides of the ice cream. Between every two banana quarters, place a whole cherry. Garnish with a spiral of whipped cream, sprinkle with chopped mixed nuts, and place another whole cherry at the top.

Skyscraper Banana Split

*L*adle 2 ounces of chocolate syrup into the bottom of a tulip glass. Add 1 scoop of vanilla ice cream. Split 1 banana lengthwise, then cut the split halves again widthwise. Put the banana quarters, cut side out, into the glass and add 1 scoop of chocolate ice cream to keep them in place. Ladle on 2 ounces of strawberry syrup. Garnish with whipped cream, and place a whole cherry at the top.

Bouquet Banana Royal

*S*lice half a banana into disks, and cover the bottom of an ice cream bowl with them. Top with 1 scoop each of vanilla, chocolate, and strawberry ice cream. Slice the rest of the banana into disks, and arrange them around the ice cream. Ladle on 2 ounces of crushed pineapple. Sprinkle with chopped mixed nuts, garnish with whipped cream, and place a whole cherry at the top.

As for David Strickler, he enrolled in classes at the University of Pittsburgh, commuting daily by train. During the two-hour trips to and from school he found time to study, then he would work nights at the drug store. On weekends he proudly played slide trombone in the college band. Strickler earned a degree in optometry just as eyeglasses with large, round lenses and tortoiseshell frames became the fashion, and just as his Banana Split became a national phenomenon. In 1913, "Doc" Strickler became Dan Livengood's partner in the pharmacy, then, eventually, sole proprietor.

"There was never a more popular, genial, or social gentleman in Westmoreland County," says Carl Mattioli,

Two years before David Strickler invented the Banana Split, he played slide trombone in the college band.

Banana Malted Royal

Slice half a banana into disks and cover the bottom of an ice cream bowl with them. Top with 1 scoop each of vanilla and chocolate ice cream. Ladle on 2 ounces of chocolate syrup. Slice the rest of the banana into disks, and arrange them around the ice cream. Sprinkle with 1 tablespoon of malted milk powder. Garnish with whipped cream, and place a whole cherry at the top.

Black and White Sundae

Split 1 banana lengthwise and place the halves parallel on a Banana Split dish. Place 1 scoop each of vanilla and chocolate ice cream between the banana halves. Sprinkle with shredded coconut, garnish between the scoops of ice cream with whipped cream, and place a whole cherry at the top.

Comet Sundae

Split 1 banana lengthwise and place the halves parallel on a Banana Split dish. Place 1 scoop of vanilla ice cream on one end of the banana halves. Ladle 2 ounces of crushed fresh strawberries over the banana, then add 2 ounces of marshmallow creme. Skewer a whole cherry with a toothpick and stick the toothpick into the ice cream. (The ball of ice cream represents the head of the comet, while the two slices of banana represent the tail.)

"I've Got a Secret"

Though he must have grown tired of hearing himself identified as the "inventor of the Banana Split," in 1959, at the age of 78, David Strickler was persuaded to contact producers of the television show *I've Got a Secret* with his story.

"My secret is that 'I Made the First Banana Split,'" wrote Strickler. He went on to explain, "A price of $.10 was set for this item in 1904. Now it can be bought nearly all over the world and sells for as high as $1.00. I hope you will enjoy, and maybe use, my big secret to entertain the T.V. audience of your interesting program." The letter was signed "Sincerely, Dr. David E. Strickler." Although Strickler never appeared as a contestant on the show, "David Strickler" more recently became an answer on the quiz show *Jeopardy*. The question, of course, asked who invented the Banana Split.

mild-mannered curator of the Latrobe Historical Society and the person entrusted with the preservation of local history. " He was a humble man who had greatness thrust upon him."

"Fame outside of Latrobe was elusive to him," says Strickler's son, William, "but that's the way Dad would have wanted it." William remembers his dad as witty and charming, with a determined manner. "He believed that it is through striving that people realize their best selves and create their most lasting contributions."

"Strickler was a hero of mine," proclaims Joseph Greubel, owner of the Valley Dairy Ice Cream Company. Greubel's father was the original "Ice Cream Joe," a local entrepreneur who started a chain of regional ice cream shops in Latrobe in 1938.

One of Greubel's shops is at the corner of Jefferson and Chestnut Streets, not far from the site of Strickler's store, where local Banana Split legacy has not been lost on the menu. The All-American Banana Split offered at Valley Dairy is a classic recipe served with a small paper American flag at the top. However, Greubel admits,

Do the Right Thing

Herluf and Jenny Sorenson operated Sorenson's Ice Cream Parlor in Grayling, Michigan, from 1925 to 1972. There, they advanced the art of Banana Split–making with strict instructions to their employees: Only the freshest fruit was to be used, and it had to be mashed by hand, to get the juices and pulp for toppings. The largest piece of mashed fruit was to be no larger than the size of a pencil eraser. The bottom of the banana boat had to be dusted with malted milk powder before assembly of a Banana Split began, and, upon completion, shaved chocolate was to be sprinkled on top of the creation. Sorenson's instruction booklet was titled *Make It Right OR Work in the Tobacco Department*.

Cherry Banana

Split 1 banana lengthwise and place the halves on a Banana Split dish in the shape of a V. Between the arms of the V place 1 scoop of vanilla ice cream. Ladle on 2 ounces of cherry syrup. Garnish with whipped cream, and place a whole cherry at the top.

Washington Monument Sundae

Split 1 banana widthwise, and cut one of the halves into disks. Ladle 1 ounce of chocolate syrup into a tall goblet, then add 1 scoop of vanilla ice cream. Ladle on 1 ounce of raspberry syrup, then add a few banana disks and 1 ounce of wet walnuts (see sidebar, page 28). Repeat until the goblet is full. When finished layering the ingredients, place the remaining half of banana vertically in a mound of whipped cream. Decorate with red and blue candy sprinkles, place whole cherries around the rim of the goblet, and stick a small American flag at the top.

Banana Sandwich

On a long dish place 1 flattened portion of vanilla ice cream. Split 1 banana lengthwise, place the halves parallel on the ice cream, and ladle on 2 ounces of cherry syrup. Place another flattened portion of vanilla ice cream on top of the banana halves. Garnish with a spiral of whipped cream, and arrange whole cherries at each corner of the top portion of ice cream.

Key Words

Ripe. A properly ripened banana, firm and plump with robust banana flavor and sweet aroma, has lost its green tinge and is just beginning to show tiny brown spots ("wearing its spotted pajamas"). Once ripened, it has about two days of optimum edibility. To keep the banana from ripening further, store it in the refrigerator. The skin will turn dark brown, but the flesh will remain firm and white for several more days.

he has discontinued the Un-Banana Split, a banana-less sundae once listed on the menu "for folks who don't like to monkey around."

"Those who had the fortune of meeting [Strickler] will never forget the experience, but those who knew him also carry a powerful memory," says Greubel wistfully. "I regret that I never had a photograph taken with him—some of his genius might have rubbed off on me."

The measure of David Strickler's life was open for all to see, yet he preferred to think of himself as a "little man." He made a profession out of a business and art out of a profession. And, even when he toiled well into his seventies, his skills behind the soda fountain remained strong. Upon retirement he stayed active in his beloved Rotary Club and enjoyed sport hunting and fishing. At the ripe old age of 80, Strickler realized a long-held dream and joined a group of close friends who chartered an airplane for an around-the-world adventure. William still has postcards his father sent from Singapore, Athens, and

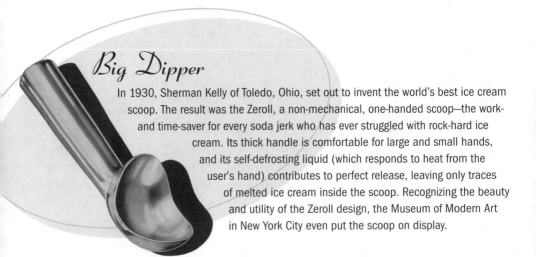

Big Dipper

In 1930, Sherman Kelly of Toledo, Ohio, set out to invent the world's best ice cream scoop. The result was the Zeroll, a non-mechanical, one-handed scoop—the work- and time-saver for every soda jerk who has ever struggled with rock-hard ice cream. Its thick handle is comfortable for large and small hands, and its self-defrosting liquid (which responds to heat from the user's hand) contributes to perfect release, leaving only traces of melted ice cream inside the scoop. Recognizing the beauty and utility of the Zeroll design, the Museum of Modern Art in New York City even put the scoop on display.

Fountain Service

"A Banana Split requires the employment of a long glass or silver dish of a size sufficient to take the whole length of the fruit with a small space to spare at either end, and of a width to allow the two halves of the banana being placed point to point, so forming an oval figure." (*The Confectioners' Handbook*, 1936)

YOU'RE MY SWEET DISH!

You're YUMMY!

"Doc" Strickler, Strickler's Drug Store, circa 1955.

Banana Chop Suey

Split 1 banana lengthwise, place the halves parallel on a Banana Split dish, and dust them with cinnamon. Place 1 scoop each of vanilla and chocolate ice cream between the banana halves. Cover the ice cream with 1 tablespoon each of wet walnuts (see sidebar), chopped figs, and crushed cherries. Garnish with whipped cream, and place a whole cherry at the top.

Cairo. After living a full life, David Strickler passed away at home on December 29, 1971.

Although others later operated the store, it retained Strickler's name. The final owner, Thomas Lazarchik, at the age of 63 and with retirement on his mind, was unable to find a successor. So at exactly 5:30 P.M. on Thursday, October 19, 2000, the doors to Strickler's Drug Store were locked forever. That day, Latrobe lost more than just a drug store. It lost a connection to American cultural history.

> **" The useful life of a Banana Split is ten minutes. "**
>
> **— Don Orlando, Director of Public Relations, St. Vincent College**

In a poignant tribute to their hometown hero, members of the local Elks Club emblazon the image of a Banana Split on their official pin, and for many years St. Vincent College has produced "Banana Split Bashes"—build-it-yourself Banana Split buffets—as part of both college orientation and alumni reunion events.

Of all those who have presided over soda fountains, perhaps no one person made a more profound contribution than David Strickler. Seldom has one man's taste-making influence paved the way for such a

Sister, Can You Spare a Banana?

During the Depression years of the 1930s, when breadlines appeared in many cities around America, New York newspapers ran the story of eight jobless young women in Manhattan who survived for more than a month by sharing only five bananas a day.

What College
Helped Create
Gene Splicing

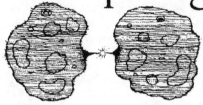

And Banana Splits?

We'll give you a couple clues. It's the one that offers some sort of financial aid to over 85% of its students. That was ranked among the top ten regional liberal arts colleges in the North.* And has over 600 medical alumni.

It's also the alma mater of Dr. Herbert Boyer, co-founder of Genentech, and inventor of gene splicing. As well as the home of the first banana split.

Those are just a few of our secrets. And we'd like to share the rest. So please call 412-537-4540 to schedule a visit. Or write "Secrets," Saint Vincent College, Latrobe, PA 15650-2690 and receive our free brochure.

Discover The Secrets Of Saint Vincent College.

*U.S. News and World Report Guide to America's Best Colleges. (1992).

culinary touchstone. It is impossible to imagine an America without the Banana Split. Strickler's brainchild was a brilliant and revolutionary recipe that not only captured the popular imagination of his time but has also endured for a century afterward.

Split Size

Ray Klavon, sporting a dark handlebar mustache, looks the part of an ice cream shopkeeper. At Klavon's Ice Cream Parlor in Pittsburgh, Pennsylvania, he serves ice cream concoctions from the soda fountain in what was once his grandfather's pharmacy. Klavon maintains the antiquated tradition of serving something salty with ice cream: he serves each dish with a round pretzel looped over the sundae spoon.

Although he still has many of the store's original Banana Split dishes, they are no longer used because of their short size. "Bananas were smaller in the old days," observes Klavon. All Banana Splits at Klavon's arrive topped with an eight-inch novelty toothpick holding a miniature monkey on a palm tree.

Turtle Split

Split 1 banana lengthwise and place the halves parallel on a Banana Split dish. Place 1 scoop each of vanilla and chocolate ice cream between the banana halves. Ladle 2 ounces of hot caramel over the vanilla and 2 ounces of hot fudge over the chocolate ice cream. Add whole buttered pecans, garnish with whipped cream, and place a whole cherry at the top.

Over the Rainbow Split

Split 1 banana lengthwise and place the halves parallel on a Banana Split dish. Place 1 scoop of vanilla ice cream between the banana halves. To the left of the vanilla place 1 scoop of orange sherbet, and to the right place 1 scoop of rainbow sherbet. Ladle 2 ounces of strawberry topping over the orange sherbet, 2 ounces of crushed pineapple over the vanilla ice cream, and 2 ounces of crushed cherries over the rainbow sherbet. Garnish with whipped cream, sprinkle with chopped mixed nuts, and place a whole cherry at the top. At one end of the "rainbow" place three chocolate "coins" wrapped in gold foil.

Chapter 3

Second Banana

> **❝ Every man is a borrower and a mimic. ❞**
> **— Ralph Waldo Emerson**

Success, it is sometimes said, is knowing what to imitate. In Wilmington, Ohio, 275 miles west of Latrobe, Pennsylvania, folks grew up hearing a story that confirmed *their* hometown as the Banana Split's birthplace. Local restaurateur E. R. "Brady" Hazard, Wilmingtonians say, never heard of David Strickler or his invention.

The winters of 1905 and 1906 were not bad in Wilmington, but then came the winter of 1907. Blustery weather and deep snows hurt soda fountain business in the small town, the story goes. So Mr. Hazard held a contest among employees of his restaurant, called The Café, offering unlimited ingredients to spur an idea for a new dessert. He submitted an entry of his own—a peeled and sliced banana heaped with three scoops of ice cream, chocolate syrup, strawberry jam, pineapple bits, chopped nuts, whipped

E. R. "Brady" Hazard, circa 1945.

cream, and cherries. The winning recipe (surprise, surprise) was Hazard's own concoction.

Hazard still needed a name for his new dish, so he enlisted the opinion of his cousin, Clifton. He served the dessert to Clifton and suggested calling it a "Banana Split." Clifton, it turned out, wasn't much of a marketing whiz. He dismissed the whole idea, while cautioning that no one would ever walk in and ask for something called a Banana Split. The name did

Interior of The Café, Wilmington, Ohio, circa 1910.

Paddy Whack

Split 1 banana lengthwise and place the halves parallel on a Banana Split dish. Place 1 scoop each of vanilla and strawberry ice cream between the banana halves. Ladle 2 ounces of crushed pineapple over the vanilla and 2 ounces of strawberry topping over the strawberry ice cream. Garnish with whipped cream, sprinkle with chopped mixed nuts, and place a whole cherry at the top.

Happy Thought No. 1

Split 1 banana lengthwise and place the halves parallel on a Banana Split dish. Place 2 scoops of strawberry ice cream between the banana halves. Ladle 2 ounces of chocolate syrup over all. Garnish with whipped cream, and sprinkle with chopped mixed nuts.

Happy Thought No. 2

Split 1 banana lengthwise and place the halves parallel on a Banana Split dish. Place 2 scoops of vanilla ice cream between the banana halves. Ladle 2 ounces of chocolate syrup over all. Garnish with whipped cream, sprinkle with chopped mixed nuts, and place a whole cherry at the top.

Peeling Back History

In 1909, Charles Rudolph Walgreen opened a soda fountain along one wall of his drug store on Chicago's South Side to boost business. The fountain, with its trademark Banana Splits, proved to be a tremendous drawing card, attracting customers who might otherwise have been just as satisfied having their pharmaceutical needs fulfilled at some other drug store in the neighborhood. And some came just for the Splits. During the summer months, customers would often surround the soda fountain counter, sometimes three or four persons deep, while Walgreens soda jerks peeled bananas and dipped ice cream.

Before she quit high school to become a showgirl, comedienne Lucille Ball worked at her hometown Walgreens store as a soda jerk; she claimed she was fired by the manager when she forgot to put the banana in a Banana Split. The founder of the Wendy's fast-food restaurant chain, Dave Thomas, also worked as a Walgreens soda jerk. He remembered the bananas, but was fired when the boss found out he wasn't 16.

Banana Split

(original Walgreens recipe)

Split 1 banana lengthwise and place the halves parallel on a Banana Split dish. Place 1 scoop of vanilla ice cream between the banana halves. To the left of the vanilla place 1 scoop of chocolate ice cream, and to the right place 1 scoop of strawberry ice cream. Ladle 2 ounces of crushed pineapple over the vanilla, 2 ounces of chocolate syrup over the chocolate, and 2 ounces of strawberry topping over the strawberry ice cream. Garnish with whipped cream. Sprinkle with chopped mixed nuts and shavings of chocolate bark. Place three stemmed cherries at the top, and arrange 2 Nabisco wafers at either end. Serve with a long-handled spoon.

stick, of course, and the visual motif of bananas and ice cream proved to be an irresistible attraction to the students from nearby Wilmington College, no matter the weather.

At first blush, the tale of Brady Hazard has a ring of authenticity. Facts get in the way, however, since he apparently served his "new" dessert in those specially designed dishes that were originally produced for David Strickler. The gentleman from Latrobe had already been there and done that.

Even in the face of overwhelming evidence proving that Hazard was three years too late, Wilmingtonians will not be disabused of the notion that their man and his version of the

Floradora

Split 1 banana lengthwise, then cut the split halves again widthwise. Place 1 scoop of strawberry ice cream on a flat dish and surround it with the banana quarters. Ladle 2 ounces of strawberry topping over all. Garnish with whipped cream, and sprinkle with chopped mixed nuts.

Old Glory Sundae

Place 2 ounces of crushed pineapple in a high-stemmed goblet. Add 1 scoop of strawberry ice cream, then 1 scoop of chocolate ice cream. Garnish with a large mound of whipped cream. Split 1 banana widthwise, stand one half up in the whipped cream, and stick an American flag on top of the banana.

Candidate's Special

Split 1 banana lengthwise and place the halves parallel on a Banana Split dish. Place 1 scoop each of vanilla and strawberry ice cream between the banana halves. Ladle 2 ounces of chocolate syrup over all. Sprinkle with whole walnuts, garnish with whipped cream, and place a whole cherry at the top.

Splitsville

Aurora, Illinois, is a city with a heightened ice cream sensibility, and one of its many ice cream shops is actually christened "The Banana Split." Randy and Lisa Brown and their staff know how to serve good malts and shakes, sodas and sundaes from their walk-up window across from Garfield Park. But what they do best is honor the name of their place with three sizes of the classic Banana Split, each made with three flavors of soft-serve ice cream. The Banana Split's Banana Splits come in small, large, and the self-explanatory "Groaner."

Banana Split were first. So exuberant are the town's proclamations regarding its culinary heritage that Wilmington throws a big summertime party—called, of course, the Banana Split Festival.

The festival had its humble beginnings in 1995, the brainstorm of local attorney Judy Gano, who believed there were a large number of people who would make a pilgrimage to the place where, ahem, the Banana Split was born. And, besides, the town needed to fund a new playground.

Plaza Square Dessert

Split 1 banana lengthwise, then cut the split halves again widthwise. Place the banana quarters on a dish in the shape of a square, with the ends crossing. Place 1 scoop of vanilla ice cream in the center of the square. Alternately place 4 slices of a peach and 4 slices of an orange around the ice cream. Top the ice cream with whipped cream and a whole red cherry. On the four corners of the banana square, place small rosettes of whipped cream and top with green cherries.

Submarine Sundae

Place 1 scoop of vanilla ice cream in the center of a Banana Split dish. Split 1 banana lengthwise, then cut the split halves again widthwise. Place 2 banana quarters to the right of the ice cream, and the remaining quarters to the left. In the center of the ice cream place a pirouette cookie to represent a periscope, and at the base on each side place 2 licorice "cigarettes," cut in two to represent guns, on top of the banana quarters. At each end place a small American flag.

W. S. Hart Sundae

Place a thin slice of chocolate cake on a fancy plate. Center 1 scoop of vanilla ice cream on the cake, cover with 2 tablespoons of wet walnuts (see sidebar on page 28), and garnish with a small rosette of whipped cream. Split 1 banana lengthwise, then cut the split halves again widthwise. Use 3 banana quarters to form a triangle around the cake. Where the ends meet, place small rosettes of whipped cream. Sprinkle with chopped mixed nuts, place small, red, heart-shaped candies on the rosettes, and stick a small American flag at the top.

Banana Capital

Until the advent of mechanically refrigerated railroad cars, Fulton, Kentucky, was a major distribution point for most of the bananas sold in the eastern United States. Bananas were loaded into "ice reefers" belonging to the Fruit Growers Express Company in New Orleans and shipped northward until they reached Fulton. At that point the cars needed to have a fresh supply of block ice to prevent spoilage. At Fulton, the long Fruit Growers Express (FGE) trains were also broken down and shipped north by the Illinois Central Railroad and east by the Louisville and Nashville Railroad.

Fulton became known as the Banana Capital of the United States. Although the days of mile-long FGE trains are long gone, for many years the city held a weeklong "International Banana Festival," with a carnival, a beauty contest (for the title of International Banana Princess), and a one-ton batch of banana pudding. The last festival was held in September 1992.

From that epiphany grew a burst of ideas, including craft and collectible exhibits, carnival games, a vintage car cruise-in, a generous outpouring of rock 'n' roll from oldies groups, and a Banana Split booth.

The booth, of course, is at center stage of the folksy event, providing attendees with delightful versions of the classic dessert. But more fascinating than the Splits themselves are the community volunteers who staff the assembly line.

Up front is Jack Powell, operating the cash register. He's a good choice for the job, since Jack happens to be president of the local bank. In charge of ice cream dipping is Alicia Smith, a high school student, recruited from her part-time job at the local ice cream shop. She moves with the agility and precision of a ballerina, her practiced fingers plying the dippers. Dean Feldmeyer, pastor of the local Methodist church, assists, as he

Cracking the Code

Hard-pressed soda fountain employees once used many numerical codes to communicate quickly among themselves. If a soda jerk "86'd" a menu item, it meant he was out of it. A call of "95" would be an alert to co-workers that a customer was walking out without paying the bill. The code "99" meant the manager was prowling about, and "98" referred to the assistant manager. A "33" was the order for a cherry-flavored Coke, "55" meant a root beer, and "19" was a Banana Split.

Panama Surprise

Place 2 scoops of vanilla ice cream on a Banana Split dish. Top with 6 pieces of cut orange and 4 dashes of grape juice. Split 1 banana lengthwise and press the halves against either side of the ice cream. Garnish with whipped cream, and place a whole cherry at the top.

Delmonico Sundaee

Split 1 banana lengthwise and place the halves parallel on a Banana Split dish. Place 2 scoops of vanilla ice cream between the banana halves. Ladle 2 ounces of chocolate syrup over one scoop and 2 ounces of coffee syrup over the other. Garnish with whipped cream.

Banana Rainbow Sundae

Split 1 banana lengthwise and place the halves parallel on a Banana Split dish. Place 1 scoop each of pistachio and strawberry ice cream between the banana halves. Along each side of the dish make a row of segments of a small, peeled, seedless orange. Garnish with whipped cream, and sprinkle with chopped pistachio nuts.

Split the Atom

Tom Levkulic is an engineer-turned-restaurateur who delights in building Atomic Banana Splits at his family's Dutch Kitchen in Frackville, Pennsylvania. The restaurant began its life as a diner, so the dessert menu steadfastly clings to the retro ice cream desserts of diner culture. The Atomic Banana Split, the brainchild of Tom's mother-in-law, Michelle Morgan, is a vertical split with a "mushroom cloud" of whipped cream.

Atomic Banana Split

Split 1 banana lengthwise and place the halves upright at opposite sides of a large goblet, forming a V. Place 1 scoop each of vanilla, chocolate, and strawberry ice cream on top of one another between the banana halves. Ladle 2 ounces of hot fudge and 2 ounces of crushed strawberries over the ice cream. Garnish with whipped cream, sprinkle with crushed peanuts, and place a whole cherry at the top.

> **I have long felt that any reviewer who expresses rage and loathing for a novel is preposterous. He or she is like a person who has put on a full suit of armor and attacked a hot fudge sundae or a Banana Split.**
>
> — **Kurt Vonnegut, Jr.**

points out, "where the artistry comes into play." After patrons help themselves from the selection of colorful toppings, he decorates their creations with whipped cream, nuts, and cherries. At the last stop is official banana splitter and former county commissioner Dave Bailey, who, in his words, "adds the health food" to finish each dessert.

By mid-afternoon, with lines growing ever longer, the volunteers' jobs demand grace under pressure. By the end of the day, they still manage to have stunning smiles for each customer. This is a labor of love for every one of the volunteers.

The festival has found a mass audience, attracting both ice cream fanatics and the idly curious to a pleasant early-summer diversion. The town of 12,000 swells to 20,000 on the first weekend in June. Seldom have capitalism and history come together so successfully. Reconnecting with folklore was a boon to the kids of Wilmington: by the second year of the event their playground had become a reality.

Boston Banana Sundae

Split 1 banana lengthwise and place the halves parallel on a Banana Split dish. Place 1 scoop each of vanilla and coffee ice cream between the banana halves. Spoon 2 ounces of crushed strawberries over the vanilla and 2 ounces of marshmallow creme over the coffee ice cream. Garnish with whipped cream, sprinkle with chopped mixed nuts, and place a whole cherry at the top.

Chaplin Charlie

Split 1 banana widthwise, and stand a piece up at each end of a flat dish. Place 1 scoop of strawberry ice cream in the center of the dish. Ladle 2 ounces of chocolate syrup over the ice cream. Over each upright banana place a touch of marshmallow creme, and sprinkle ground roasted peanuts over all.

Banana Cut-Up

In the center of a Banana Split dish place 1 scoop each of vanilla, chocolate, and strawberry ice cream. Ladle 3 ounces of chocolate syrup over all. Slice half a banana into disks, place them all around the ice cream, and sprinkle with walnuts.

Banana Walk

Split 1 banana lengthwise and place the halves parallel on a Banana Split dish. Place 2 scoops of vanilla ice cream between the banana halves, and ladle 1 ounce of butterscotch topping over each scoop. Garnish with whipped cream, sprinkle with shredded coconut, and place a whole cherry at the top.

Yes, We Have No Bonanza

At the beginning of the 20th century the North Pole beckoned as a challenge to explorers. Reaching the pole was viewed as a measure of man's highest abilities, just as reaching the moon provided a similar challenge during the 1960s. But in 1909, while Robert E. Peary and Frederick A. Cook were arguing over who got there first, soda jerks were already making a Banana Split to celebrate the heroic achievement.

North Pole Sundae

Split 1 large banana lengthwise, and arrange the halves on a long plate to represent the runners of a sleigh. On these, place 1 large scoop of vanilla ice cream to represent a "pack," and to simulate snow, cover the "pack" with marshmallow creme. On one end of the plate place a small candy polar bear; at the other end, place 6 jelly gum drops. On top of the ice cream stick a small American flag.

> **Most historians agree—Latrobe is the home of the Banana Split.**
>
> — **Bryce Thomson,**
> ***Sundae School Newsletter***

> **I belonged in Idle Valley like a pearl onion on a Banana Split.**
>
> — From ***The Long*** Goodbye
> by Raymond Chandler

As for the basis of the local legend, Ms. Gano, a former city attorney and candidate for municipal court judge, seems to equivocate. "I guess you could say that, at least in my heart, I believe our town was first," she says.

So how does she explain Latrobe's earlier claim? "They may have gotten their date wrong," speculates Ms. Gano.

Kay Fisher, curator of the Clinton County Historical Society, is more cautious about the controversy. She says that the Banana Split was "supposedly" invented in Wilmington. "We deal in history," says Ms. Fisher. "Unless someone shows me proof or documentation, it's more correct to use the term 'supposedly.'"

But Mary Gibson shares none of the doubt. She was born in Wilmington and grew up just a few doors down from what

Maraschino. The eternally popular cherry is pitted, sugar-pickled, almond-flavored, then dyed with red food coloring before being perched demurely at the summit of an ice cream concoction.

Split Second

The success of the original Banana Split provoked hordes of imitators besides Brady Hazard. In 1906 Stinson Thomas, head soda fountain clerk at Butler's Department Store in Boston, began serving a version that included banana halves topped with two small scoops of vanilla ice cream, sliced peaches, and pistachios. Gus Napoulos was splitting bananas at the Elite Confectionery in Davenport, Iowa, the same year. And Letty Lally offered an early concoction of bananas and ice cream at the soda fountain of Foeller's Drug Store in Columbus, Ohio, as early as 1907. Ms. Lally called her dessert the "Five-Six-Seven."

Split the Profits

The seaside city of Nha Trang, Vietnam, of all places, has 2 Banana Split Cafés. Even more interesting, they are located side by side, yet have different owners.

is now Gibson's Goodies, where they've served handmade ice cream to local folks for over 60 years. It was a bakery that old Charley Semler turned into an ice cream store during World War II, and she inherited his first-hand recipes for 40 or so of the best flavors. "As for the Banana Split, our town took claim to it first," she says with a straight face, "so that makes us first—case closed."

Gibson's provides all the ice cream for the Banana Split Festival: 556 gallons, to be exact. To that add 14 gallons of maraschino cherries, 100 pounds of peanuts, 15 canisters of whipped cream, 25 No. 10 cans each of chocolate syrup, crushed pineapple, caramel, and strawberry toppings, and 4200 bananas, and you have the makings for all the Banana Splits consumed during the two-day event.

H. L. Mencken once asserted that a legend is "a lie that has attained the dignity of age," and that probably explains why the story of Brady Hazard's ice cream fountain is stubbornly

Banana Splits and Sundaes
Choices

TOPPINGS	ICE CREAM
Strawberry	Vanilla
Chocolate	Strawberry
Pineapple	Chocolate
Caramel	

INCLUDES WHIPPED CREAM, NUTS & A CHERRY

3 DIP BANANA SPLIT OR SUNDAE	$4.00
2 DIP BANANA SPLIT OR SUNDAE	$3.00
1 DIP BANANA SPLIT OR SUNDAE	$2.00
2 DIPS OF ICE CREAM	$2.00
1 DIP OF ICE CREAM	$1.25

Single dips of Vanilla Ice Cream available
at the Pepsi/Root Beer Float Booth

" The world divides into two great camps: Banana Split lovers and infidels. "

— Pat Larrick, chairman of the Banana Split Festival in Wilmington, Ohio

kept alive by the good folks in Wilmington. Actually, Hazard closed his restaurant in the early 1920s and went to work for the Ohio Power and Light Company, where he supervised right-of-way purchases for the utility. He eventually moved to Columbus, where he served as a lobbyist for the power company in the state legislature. To the best of his family's recollection, he never made another Banana Split.

Hazard's grandson, Daniel Rodenfels, publisher of *The Logan Daily News*, in Logan, Ohio, says he has been asked many times whether his mother's father was indeed responsi-

Ripe Old Age

Time has stood still inside the Pioneer Drug Store on Main Street in Elk Point, South Dakota. Tulip sundaes and ice cream concoctions are still prepared at Edgar Schmiedt's marble soda fountain, installed circa 1906, by Edgar's granddaughter, Barb Wurtz. Three versions of the Banana Split still smother local taste buds at a fountain that is almost as old as the Banana Split itself.

The Rocket

Place 1 scoop of chocolate ice cream in a tall ice cream soda goblet, and ladle on 2 ounces of chocolate syrup. Add 1 scoop of vanilla ice cream, and ladle on 2 ounces of crushed pineapple. Finally, add 1 scoop of strawberry ice cream, and ladle on 2 ounces of crushed strawberries. Split 1 banana lengthwise, then cut the split halves lengthwise again. Stick the banana spears around the inside of the glass, with the pointed ends protruding over the top. Garnish with whipped cream, and place a whole cherry at the top.

Triple Treat

Split 1 banana lengthwise and place the halves parallel on a Banana Split dish. Place 1 scoop each of rocky road, cherry nut, and vanilla ice cream between the banana halves. Ladle 2 ounces of caramel syrup over the rocky road, 2 ounces of chocolate syrup over the cherry nut, and 2 ounces of crushed strawberries over the vanilla ice cream. Garnish with whipped cream, and place a whole cherry at the top.

Black & White Fantasy

Split 1 banana lengthwise and place the halves parallel on a Banana Split dish. Place 1 scoop each of vanilla, chocolate, and chocolate chip ice cream between the banana halves. Spoon 2 ounces of hot fudge over the vanilla, 2 ounces of marshmallow creme over the chocolate, and 2 ounces of chocolate syrup over the chocolate chip ice cream. Garnish with whipped cream, and place a whole cherry at the top.

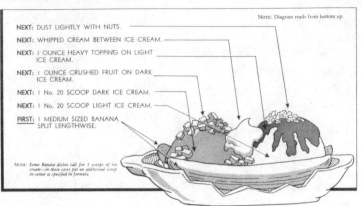

NOTE: Diagram reads from bottom up.

NEXT: DUST LIGHTLY WITH NUTS.

NEXT: WHIPPED CREAM BETWEEN ICE CREAM.

NEXT: 1 OUNCE HEAVY TOPPING ON LIGHT ICE CREAM.

NEXT: 1 OUNCE CRUSHED FRUIT ON DARK ICE CREAM.

NEXT: 1 No. 20 SCOOP DARK ICE CREAM.

NEXT: 1 No. 20 SCOOP LIGHT ICE CREAM.

FIRST: 1 MEDIUM SIZED BANANA SPLIT LENGTHWISE.

NOTE: Some Banana dishes call for 3 scoops of ice cream—in these cases put an additional scoop in center as specified in formula.

ble for inventing the Banana Split. "Who knows?" says Rodenfels. "And who cares?"

Any quibbles come as afterthoughts. Say what you will about its dubious history, there is something redemptive in the portrait of Americana on display at the Banana Split Festival. There is love of country in every serving of bananas and ice cream, helping to further an appreciation of a national treasure. Visitors who come with scant knowledge of the dessert's true genesis are content to devour their Banana Splits, enjoy the entertainment, and bask in the warmth of small-town hospitality.

Imitation is said to be the sincerest form of flattery, but in the case of Wilmington, Ohio, and its Banana Split, the festival is an even greater tribute.

Souper Bowl

Since the 1950s, Tom's Ice Cream Bowl in Zanesville, Ohio, has stubbornly refused to serve sundaes in traditional fountainware. So expect your Banana Split to come in an old-fashioned Buffalo China soup bowl, with three scoops of ice cream piled on top of one another, surrounded by a banana sliced into disks. Toppings include crushed cherries, pineapple, marshmallow, and Tom's famous freshly roasted nuts.

In 1941, *Drug Store Management* scolded fountain operators for permitting the use of slang in their establishments, pointing out that "it tends to reduce the formality of the occasion and may perhaps suggest a lack of respect for the customer's order." Saying "Burn one with a cackle," to refer to an egg malted milk and using the phrase "farmer's lunch" for a Banana Split were equally inappropriate in the judgment of the article's authors.

" Eat around the banana, Dad. It's just empty vitamins. "

**— Bart explaining the secret to eating
a Banana Split to Homer on
the TV show *The Simpsons***

Split Ends

Bananas are properly peeled from the non-stem end. This leaves most of the "strings" attached to the skin, obviating the need to remove them separately, and this method allows the stem end to be used as a handle.

SUIT THE *Color* TO THE *Use*

TIPPED WITH GREEN?

The banana is partially ripe. The pulp is firm, starchy, slightly tart. Just ready to bake or broil or fry —cooking brings out a different, delicious flavor.

ALL YELLOW?

Now it's ready to eat or cook and use as an ingredient in baking.

FLECKED WITH BROWN?

Now it's fully ripe, at its best for eating, infant feeding and as an ingredient in baking. It's sweet, mellow, thoroughly digestible and delicious in fruit cups, salads, desserts and milk shakes.

Chapter 4

The Banana Metaphor

> **❝** Is that a banana in your pocket, or are you glad to see me? **❞**
>
> — Mae West

Of all the adjectives one might think to apply to Carmen Miranda, *boring* would rank somewhere near the bottom of the list. The perpetual-motion machine from Brazil burst into Hollywood in the late 1930s, wrapped in outrageous costumes including turbans topped with bananas and other exotic fruits. She sang and samba-ed her way to stardom as a fiery, language-mangling, oversexed Latina. By 1940 she was the highest-paid woman in America.

Carmen Miranda was short and curvy, with dark, wavy hair. The magazine *Classic Images* described her as having a "Bob Hope ski-slope nose," a huge, infectious grin, and eyes "like two green headlights." Early in her career as a singer she adopted the gaudy headgear, bangles, and exposed midriffs of Brazilian street vendors, overtly sexual, but in a playful way.

Her tutti-frutti hats reached unparalleled heights of camp lunacy in films like *The Gang's All Here*, a trippy 1943 Busby Berkeley Technicolor extravaganza with Alice Faye, Eugene Pallette, Edward Everett Horton, and the Benny Goodman Orchestra. For European audiences the movie title was changed to *Banana Split*, since the dessert was by then universally synonymous with America.

The film features scores of scantily clad chorus girls dancing with eight-foot-long bananas on a tropical-fruit plantation, accompanied by Carmen, wearing an enormous hat composed of thousands of fruit prod-

Split Image

Andy Warhol is famous for the explicit sexualizing of the banana on the cover of the Velvet Underground's 1967 record album, and for developing the rock group's marketing slogan, "Unzip a banana." When you peeled off the banana on the cover, a pink banana would show up inside.

" I would rather play 'Chiquita Banana' and have my swimming pool, than play Bach and starve. "

— Xavier Cugat

Carmen Miranda

Ice Cream Corner, North Clearwater, Florida

Split 1 banana lengthwise and place the halves parallel on a Banana Split dish. Place 2 scoops of coconut ice cream between the banana halves. Ladle 3 ounces of rum-spiked crushed pineapple over all. Garnish with whipped cream, and place a whole cherry at the top.

"Sure Thing" Banana Split

Elaine's on Franklin, Chapel Hill, North Carolina

Split 1 banana lengthwise and place the halves parallel on a Banana Split dish. Place 1 scoop each of mint, strawberry, and white chocolate ice cream between the banana halves. Ladle 3 ounces of rum-spiked crushed pineapple over all. Garnish with whipped cream, and sprinkle with chopped walnuts.

Mango Banana Split

India, Warren, Rhode Island

Split 1 banana lengthwise and place the halves parallel on an oval platter. Place 3 scoops of mango ice cream in between the banana halves. Ladle 2 ounces of mango pulp over the first scoop, 2 ounces of chocolate syrup over the second, and 2 ounces of crushed pineapple over the third. Sprinkle with toasted cashews and golden raisins, and place a whole cherry at the top of each scoop of ice cream.

Dirty Dancing

American-born cabaret performer Josephine Baker caused a sensation at the Folies Bergère in Paris in 1926 by dancing on a mirror—nude except for a string of plush bananas swathed around her waist. Soon, banana-clad starlets began turning up everywhere.

❝ Man is like a banana. Strong and firm, bright and phallic, and he's protected by his all-important shield. But when a woman comes along, you know, she sees this bright phallic beast and she wants it. So she starts peeling away your all-important shield. First, she wants to see your romantic side, then she wants to see your passionate side, finally she wants to see your soft, caring, feminine side. She keeps peeling and peeling until you're left there buck naked. ❞

— Edward Burns as Barry, summing up relationships in the film *The Brothers McMullen* while peeling a banana

Scent of a Banana

The Smell and Taste Treatment and Research Foundation conducted a study to determine which foods aroused each gender. The results showed that men's sexual organs were most stimulated by the aroma of pumpkin pie, while women were most aroused by that of bananas.

Banana Split

Louie's Backyard, Key West, Florida

*S*plit 1 banana lengthwise and place the halves parallel on a
Banana Split dish. Place 1 scoop each of banana-rum and dark
chocolate ice cream between the banana halves. Ladle 2 ounces of
butterscotch sauce with crushed walnuts over the banana-rum and
2 ounces of chocolate syrup over the dark chocolate ice cream. Garnish
with whipped cream, sprinkle with shaved chocolate, and place 3 griottine
cherries (small, dark red cherries marinated in kirsch) at the top.

Burnaby Street Banana Split

Barracuda Grill, Hamilton, Bermuda

*S*plit 1 native Bermuda banana lengthwise and place the halves
parallel on a Banana Split dish. Place 1 scoop each of cinnamon,
dark chocolate, and pistachio ice cream between the banana halves.
Ladle 3 ounces of white chocolate sauce over all and drizzle with warm
caramel. Garnish with whipped cream, sprinkle with a mix of chopped
hard chocolate and pistachio nuts, and place 3 caramelized cherries
(cherries sautéed in butter) at the top.

Banana Split

Mar y Sol's, Chicago, Illinois

*P*lace 1 scoop each of strawberry and pineapple sorbet on a slice of
chocolate chip–banana cake. Split 1 banana lengthwise, and cover
the halves with pecan-crunch enrobing chocolate. When the chocolate
shell hardens, press the banana halves against the sides of the sorbet.
Ladle 2 ounces of hot fudge over all, garnish with whipped cream, and
place a whole cherry at the top.

Easy to Love

Cypress Gardens, founded by Dick Pope in 1936, was Florida's first theme park, and the backdrop for such 1950s films as *Easy to Love*, the one where Esther Williams water-skis her way into Van Johnson's heart. Two of the park's signature attractions were the girls dressed as southern belles and Banana Splits at the Ice Cream Parlor. The park closed in 2003—the belles and the Splits are now only memories.

ucts. This is Berkeley at his most surreal, with giant bananas descending into a ring of oversize strawberries as the bananas in Carmen's headdress swell in size.

The "message" here is hardly subliminal. As Carmen might have said, "The cat is spilling out of the beans." A banana was never just a banana, at least not if Busby Berkeley was involved. He had a well-known fondness for sexual metaphors, but in this film it's pushed into overdrive.

Film historian David Thomson noted that the movie "contains in its opening sequence one of cinema's most breathtaking traveling shots and, at its conclusion, the endlessly erectile banana routine—lewdness has never been as merry."

"Nothing in cinema," wrote Julian Dibbell in the *Village Voice*, "has captured more accurately the North Atlantic fantasy

Tres Marias

Cien Años Mexican Grill, Oro Valley, Arizona

Split 1 banana lengthwise and place the halves parallel on a Banana Split dish. Place 1 scoop each of vanilla, chocolate, and strawberry ice cream between the banana halves. Ladle 3 ounces of chocolate syrup over all. Garnish with whipped cream, and sprinkle with slivered almonds.

Banana Split

Dragonfly, New York, New York

Split 1 banana lengthwise, and caramelize the halves in a pan over medium heat (see sidebar, page 58). Place the caramelized banana halves in an ice cream bowl and put 1 scoop each of mango, green tea, and red bean ice cream between them. Drizzle with warm chocolate syrup spiked with amaretto, and garnish with whipped cream and sliced strawberries.

Boardwalk Banana Split

Rosy's at the Beach, Morgan Hill, California

Split 1 banana lengthwise and place the halves parallel on a Banana Split dish. Place 1 scoop each of French vanilla, chocolate, and strawberry ice cream between the banana halves. Ladle 2 ounces of caramel syrup over the French vanilla, 2 ounces of hot fudge over the chocolate, and 2 ounces of crushed strawberries over the strawberry ice cream. Garnish with whipped cream, and sprinkle with toasted walnuts.

of the South as a site for innocent erotic anarchy." *Premiere* magazine called *The Gang's All Here* (a.k.a. *Banana Split*) "one of the most daring films ever made."

Sex sells. And sex sells bananas. Busby Berkeley's metaphoric appetite for the tropical fruit was not lost on Madison Avenue. In 1944, the United Fruit Company launched an ambitious advertising campaign to promote the product to postwar consumers.

Inspired by the public's infatuation with Carmen Miranda, admen created a deliciously sexy half-banana, half-woman cartoon character they baptized "Chiquita," who delivered their commercial message with a sensuous rumba rhythm: "I'm Chiquita Banana and I've come to say / Bananas have to ripen in a certain way / . . . like the climate of the very, very tropical equator / So you should never put bananas in the re-fri-ger-a-tor."

Key Words

Caramelize. To add a sweet, golden-brown crust to a banana by cooking it in melted sugar. Cook 3 ounces of granulated or brown sugar in a saucepan over medium heat until it turns a light caramel color, then add 4 slightly underripe banana halves; cook for 60 seconds, add 1 tablespoon of melted butter, and remove from heat. Place banana halves in serving dishes, and assemble with ice cream and toppings.

Soba Banana Split

Soba, Pittsburgh, Pennsylvania

Split 1 red banana (in season) lengthwise, and caramelize the halves in a pan over medium heat (see sidebar). Place the caramelized banana halves parallel on an oval dish and put 1 scoop each of vanilla-goat cheese, chocolate-pistachio, and piña colada ice cream between them. Drizzle with sweet-and-sour tamarind sauce and chocolate syrup, and sprinkle with crushed toasted cashews.

Banana Split

Zuka, Houston, Texas

Split 1 banana lengthwise and place the halves parallel on a Banana Split dish. Place 1 scoop each of coconut and blood orange ice cream between the banana halves. Ladle 2 ounces of pineapple jam over the coconut and 2 ounces of *cajeta* (Mexican caramel syrup) over the blood orange ice cream. Garnish with whipped cream, and sprinkle with toasted coconut and candied almonds.

Club Sushi Banana Split

Club Sushi, Hermosa Beach, California

Split 1 banana lengthwise and place the halves parallel on a Banana Split dish. Place 1 scoop each of vanilla, green tea, and ginger ice cream between the banana halves. Ladle 3 ounces of chocolate syrup over all. Garnish with whipped cream, and place a whole cherry at the top.

Cajun Banana Split

Yamamanem's Cajun Café, Clive, Iowa

Split 1 banana lengthwise and place the halves parallel on a Banana Split dish. Place 2 scoops of vanilla ice cream between the banana halves. Ladle 2 ounces of crushed strawberries over one scoop and 2 ounces of chocolate syrup over the other. Garnish with whipped cream, and sprinkle crumbled pralines over the top.

Caramelized Banana Split

Gautreau's, New Orleans, Louisiana

*P*lace 1 slice of banana bread on an oval plate. Split 1 banana lengthwise, and caramelize the halves in a pan over medium heat (see sidebar, page 58). Place the caramelized banana halves parallel on the banana bread, and put 2 scoops of vanilla bean ice cream between them. Ladle 2 ounces of hot fudge over one scoop and 2 ounces of hot butterscotch over the other. Garnish with whipped cream, sprinkle with toasted walnuts, and place a whole cherry at the top.

Le Banana Split

Isobel, Brooklyn, New York

*S*plit 1 banana lengthwise, and caramelize the halves in a pan over medium heat (see sidebar, page 58). Place the caramelized banana halves on an oval dish, and put 2 scoops of French vanilla ice cream between them. Drizzle with warm chocolate syrup, and sprinkle with chopped toasted walnuts.

Asqew Grilled Banana Split

Asqew Grill, San Francisco, California

*S*plit 1 unpeeled banana lengthwise and grill both sides (see sidebar, page 73). After removing the peel, place the grilled banana halves parallel on a Banana Split dish. Place 1 scoop each of vanilla, caramel, and mocha ice cream between the banana halves. Ladle 2 ounces of chocolate syrup and 2 ounces of hot caramel over all. Garnish with whipped cream, and sprinkle with caramelized almonds (almonds and sugar sautéed in butter).

Split Lips

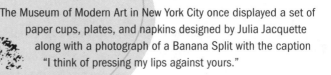

The Museum of Modern Art in New York City once displayed a set of paper cups, plates, and napkins designed by Julia Jacquette along with a photograph of a Banana Split with the caption "I think of pressing my lips against yours."

"Back when I was your age, I always made myself a big Banana Split after sex. I think you're gonna need one tonight."

— Lin Shaye as Magda, counseling Mary in the film *There's Something About Mary*

"Suppose we do a number with musical swords, and we can end up cutting Honey in half?" asks Fred.

"I'd much rather split a Banana Split three ways," replies Honey.

— Fred Astaire as Fred Ayers and Ginger Rogers as Honey Hale in the film *Flying Down to Rio*

United Colors

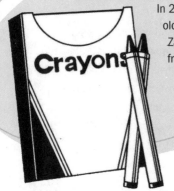

In 2002, Crayola introduced a crayon maker so kids could recycle their old crayons into solid hues or colorful swirls. According to Paul Zadorsky of Crayola, "They're wildly inspired. We're seeing everything from tie-dye 'Flower Power' crayons to a yellow-white 'Banana Split.'"

Café Banana Split

Afterwards Café, Washington, D.C.

Split 1 banana lengthwise and place the halves parallel on an oval platter. Place 1 scoop each of cinnamon, vanilla, and chocolate ice cream in between the banana halves. Ladle 3 ounces of caramel syrup over all. Garnish with whipped cream, sprinkle with cinnamon-toasted crushed walnuts (walnuts that have been sprinkled with cinnamon, toasted, and then crushed), and drizzle with raspberry puree.

Joe's Bimini Banana Split

Sloppy Joe's on the Beach, Treasure Island, Florida

Split 1 banana lengthwise, then cut the split halves again widthwise. Cover the banana quarters with enrobing chocolate. When the chocolate shell hardens, place the banana quarters upright around the edge of an oversize margarita goblet. Add 1 scoop each of vanilla, chocolate, and strawberry ice cream. Ladle 3 ounces of hot fudge over all. Garnish with whipped cream, sprinkle with chopped peanuts, and place a whole cherry at the top.

Banana Split

Noche, New York, New York

Split 1 baby banana lengthwise, and caramelize the halves in a pan over medium heat (see sidebar, page 58). Place the caramelized banana halves parallel on a round dish and put 2 scoops of vanilla ice cream between them. Place slices of mango and papaya on top of the ice cream, and ladle 3 ounces of chocolate sauce spiked with coffee liqueur over all. Garnish with whipped cream tinted with sour cherry juice, and sprinkle with milk chocolate–covered coffee beans.

Marketing guru David Ogilvy asserts, "It takes a big idea to attract the attention of consumers and get them to buy your product. Unless your advertising contains a big idea, it will pass like a ship in the night."

The banana babe got noticed in a big way. Her larger-than-life character debuted in a Technicolor film short," *Miss Chiquita Banana's Beauty Treatment*, in which she sings to revive an exhausted housewife. It captured a moment in time through the lens of advertising, and Chiquita became a celebrity in her own right. She appeared on the radio with Fred Allen, Bert Lahr, and Edgar Bergen and Charlie

Southwestern Banana Split

Café Terra Cotta, Tucson, Arizona

Split 1 banana lengthwise and coat the halves with enrobing chocolate. When the chocolate shell hardens, place the banana halves parallel on a Banana Split dish. Place 2 scoops of jalapeño-spiked vanilla ice cream between the banana halves. Ladle 3 ounces of hot fudge over all. Garnish with whipped cream, and sprinkle with chili-spiced pecans.

Banana Split

Merlot Restaurant, Duluth, Georgia

Split 1 banana lengthwise, and caramelize the halves in a pan over medium heat (see sidebar, page 58). Place the caramelized banana halves parallel on a Banana Split dish and put 1 scoop each of coffee and chocolate ice cream between them. Ladle 3 ounces of goat milk–caramel sauce over all. Garnish with whipped cream, sprinkle with chopped peanuts, and place a whole fresh strawberry at the top.

Banana Split

Jack Fry's, Louisville, Kentucky

Split 1 banana lengthwise, place the halves parallel in an almond-laced cup, and drizzle 1 ounce of cilantro syrup over the banana. Place 1 scoop each of vanilla ice cream and coconut sorbet between the banana halves. Ladle 2 ounces of butterscotch syrup over the vanilla ice cream and 2 ounces of strawberry puree over the coconut sorbet. Cover with mixed berries (fresh strawberries, blueberries, and raspberries). Garnish with whipped cream, and sprinkle with pieces of macadamia-nut brittle.

Sex and the City

Mayor Willie Brown calls San Francisco "the sexiest city in the country." Perhaps with that in mind, the folks at Max's Opera Café created an original dessert, blissfully breaking rules of propriety along the way. In what surely must be one of the most cloyingly suggestive concoctions found anywhere, the Big Banana consists of a long, whole banana, strategically placed upright in a tulip glass, with a scoop of ice cream on either side, and three different sauces impolitely oozing over the top. However, some people find the sexual imagery a bit too intimidating. Max's management was taken to city court by a woman who claimed the Big Banana left her husband impotent.

❝ I might never find a lesson in why Burger and I split, but, at least for the moment, there was a Banana Split. ❞

— Sarah Jessica Parker as Carrie Bradshaw
in HBO's *Sex and the City*

❝ Haven't you bothered me enough, you big banana-head? ❞

— Marilyn Monroe as Angela Phinlay
in the film *The Asphalt Jungle*

More Sex and the City

Virtual Pleasures, a San Francisco–based computer bulletin board, lists such social activities as the X-Rated Banana Split Contest, featuring particularly inventive uses for kiwis, bananas, strawberries, and chocolate sprinkles.

Roaring Fork Banana Split

Roaring Fork, Scottsdale, Arizona

Split 1 banana lengthwise, roll the halves in cinnamon and sugar, wrap them in flour tortillas, then deep-fry at 375° F. Place the banana "tortillas" parallel on an oval plate and put 2 scoops of Ben & Jerry's Chunky Monkey ice cream between them. Ladle 3 ounces of chocolate syrup over all. Garnish with whipped cream, and sprinkle with slivered almonds.

Waffle Banana Split

Cafeteria, New York, New York

Make 1 waffle using basic waffle mix, coating the waffle iron very well with butter. Split 1 banana lengthwise, and caramelize the halves in a pan over medium heat (see sidebar, page 58). Place the caramelized banana halves parallel on the waffle. Place 1 scoop each of vanilla, chocolate, and strawberry ice cream on top of the banana halves. Garnish with whipped cream, then drizzle with caramel and chocolate sauces. Place a whole cherry at the top, and sprinkle with powdered sugar.

Bossa-Style Banana Split

Bossa, Houston, Texas

Split 1 banana lengthwise, then split each half lengthwise again. Season the banana spears with cinnamon and sugar, wrap each in a 10 x 10-inch egg roll wrapper, and deep-fry at 375° F. Line the inside of a molded chocolate cup (available at gourmet food stores) with chocolate ganache. Place 1 large scoop of coconut gelato in the cup, and ladle on 2 ounces of sweet pineapple chutney. Arrange the banana spears on the top in a cross-hatch pattern.

McCarthy. Her 60-second ditty was played on the radio, on juke-boxes, and by the big bands. It was performed by Xavier Cugat, Buddy Clark, the King Sisters, even by Carmen Miranda herself.

Time magazine called Chiquita Banana "Number One on the jingle-jangle hit parade." College men voted Chiquita "the girl they'd most like to get in a refrigerator with."

Sex gave the banana allure—the purchase of bananas was promoted against the backdrop of barely restrained sexual fantasy and the sultry tropics. And Americans responded.

Oral History

In January 1998, Las Vegas stripper Hayley Huntington almost choked to death on a ripe banana at a Deep Throat contest in a topless club.

Split at the Seams

"Candy Pants," the edible underwear invented in the 1960s, were available in three flavors: Wild Cherry, Hot Chocolate, and Banana Split.

Banana Split

Café Sol, Christ Church, Barbados

Split 1 banana lengthwise and place the halves parallel on a Banana Split dish. Place 1 scoop each of vanilla, chocolate, and coconut ice cream between the banana halves. Ladle 3 ounces of chocolate syrup over all. Garnish with whipped cream, and sprinkle with chopped mixed nuts.

Tsunami Banana Split

Tsunami, East Hampton, New York

Split 1 banana lengthwise, dip the halves into tempura batter (see sidebar, page 72), and flash-fry quickly on both sides in very hot oil. Place the fried banana halves parallel on a Banana Split dish and put 2 scoops of Tahitian vanilla ice cream between them. Ladle 2 ounces of chocolate syrup over one scoop and 2 ounces of peanut butter sauce over the other. Garnish with whipped cream, and sprinkle with shaved chocolate.

Hot Banana Split

Tequila Joe's, Manila, Philippines

Line a microwave-safe Banana Split dish with graham cracker crumbs. Place 6 large marshmallows in two rows at the center of the dish, and sprinkle them with grated semisweet chocolate. Split 1 banana lengthwise and place the halves parallel over the marshmallows. Heat in a microwave oven for about 20 seconds. Remove from oven, place 2 scoops of vanilla ice cream between the banana halves, sprinkle with chopped pistachios, and drizzle with chocolate syrup and crème de menthe.

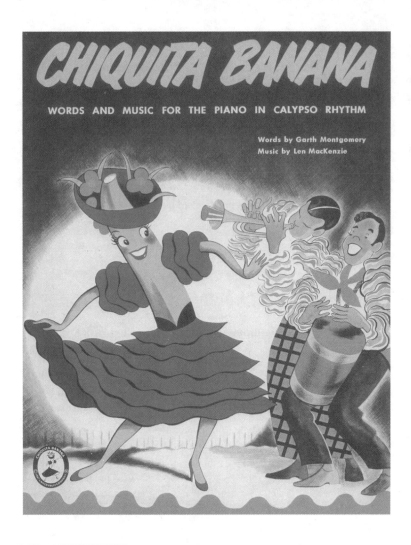

CHIQUITA BANANA

WORDS AND MUSIC FOR THE PIANO IN CALYPSO RHYTHM

Words by Garth Montgomery
Music by Len MacKenzie

Simulated Sex

A teacher at Gulf Coast High School in Naples, Florida, was dismissed for giving a condom demonstration with a banana, mood lighting, and Christmas carols playing in the background.

Betty Jimenez has studied the relationship between food and sex, and in an article called "The Forbidden Fruit" (Suite101.com, October 2000) she wrote: "We all know, from those Hollywood sex scenes, that food, as erotic foreplay, is fun, and fantasy. After all, when we see ads of women eating bananas suggestively, the implication and comparison is all too red-hot clear."

Several cultures regard the banana as an erotic stimulant because of its phallic resemblance. British schoolchildren are

Samui Banana Split

Blue Lagoon, Ko Samui, Thailand

Split 1 banana lengthwise and place the halves parallel on a Banana Split dish. Place 2 scoops of coconut ice cream between the banana halves. Ladle 3 ounces of strawberry sauce over all. Garnish with whipped cream, and sprinkle with fried cashews and toasted black sesame seeds.

As Good As It Gets

Restaurant critic Ted Scheffler of the *Salt Lake City Weekly* enthusiastically recommends the Tempura Banana Split at The Happy Sumo, "where the hot tempura–fried banana commingles with cold vanilla ice cream in a way that I could only use sexual terms to describe. Let's just say, it makes me moan."

Tempura Banana Split

Line the bottom of a Banana Split dish with a crust made of crushed chocolate-chip cookies. Split 1 banana lengthwise, dip the halves into tempura batter (see sidebar, page 72), and flash-fry quickly on both sides in very hot oil. Place the banana halves parallel in the dish (on top of the crust), then place 3 scoops of vanilla ice cream between the halves. Ladle 3 ounces of chocolate syrup over all, and garnish with whipped cream.

A Split from Tradition

The seductive "V" of Cold Stone Creamery's house-made waffle cones is called "cone cleavage." What you put into your cone at any of the nearly 1,000 specialty ice cream parlors is limited only by your own imagination, and every visit provides another chance to add ingredients like a kid adding ornaments to a Christmas tree. Your choice of basic ice cream is plopped onto a frozen granite stone, and then you select from a smorgasbord of fruits, nuts, candies, and other good stuff you want "smushed in" to create a personalized ice cream. One of Cold Stone Creamery's own formulas, Banana Splitacular, includes sliced bananas, pineapple, fudge, roasted almonds, cherry pie filling, and whipped cream—all mixed into Sweet Cream ice cream.

Tempura Batter

1 cup flour
½ teaspoon baking powder
1 egg
1 cup ice water

Sift the flour and baking powder together. Mix the egg and ice water in a bowl, then add the flour mixture. Blend just until the dry ingredients are moistened. Dip the banana halves into the batter.

Tempura Banana Split

Nikai Sushi, Jackson, Wyoming

Split 1 banana lengthwise, dip the halves into tempura batter (see sidebar), and flash-fry quickly on both sides in very hot oil. Place the fried banana halves parallel on a Banana Split dish and put 3 scoops of toasted-coconut ice cream between them. Ladle 2 ounces of chocolate syrup over the first scoop, 2 ounces of caramel syrup over the second, and 2 ounces of raspberry puree over the third. Garnish with whipped cream, and crumble a chocolate-chip cookie over the top.

" Venus with Jupiter is too much of a good thing, like a double Banana Split. "

— Eleanor Buckwalter, astrologist

First Lady of Fruit

Miss Chiquita Banana came to life in 1944 from the pen of Dik Browne, the same artist who gave the world the cartoon strip *Hi and Lois*. She was depicted as part banana until 1987, when artist Oscar Grillo, the famous animator, transformed her into a woman.

Thrill of the Grill

To grill a banana for a Grilled Banana Split, preheat the grill to medium-high heat. With the banana still in its skin, split it lengthwise and brush the cut sides with melted butter. Place the cut (flat) side down on the grill, and cook for 4 to 6 minutes (or until edges begin to bubble). Turn over and cook for 2 or 3 more minutes, or until lightly browned. Let the banana cool slightly, then remove the skins. Place the banana halves in a serving dish and assemble the Split with ice cream and toppings.

Grilled Banana Split

Meritage, East Greenwich, Rhode Island

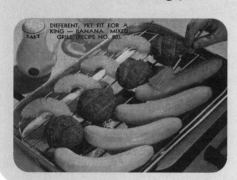

Split 1 unpeeled banana lengthwise and grill both sides (see sidebar). After removing the peel, place the grilled banana halves parallel on a Banana Split dish. Place 3 scoops of vanilla ice cream between the banana halves, and ladle 3 ounces of chocolate syrup over all. Garnish with whipped cream, and sprinkle with chopped toasted walnuts.

> **Hokay! Theese time, make weeth the careful! Knock one banana off my head and I will make you the flat pancake!**
>
> — **Carmen Miranda to director Busby Berkeley after an unfortunate accident with the camera rigging knocked her sky-high headpiece to the ground in a scramble of bananas and strawberries**

Shagadelic Split

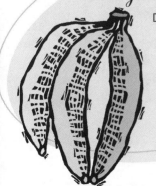

During the opening credits of the first Austin Powers movie sequel, *The Spy Who Shagged Me*, the British secret agent cavorts through a hotel in the nude with his private parts surreptitiously blocked from view by various phallic items—from a rump roast to a Banana Split.

Key Words

Banana Hammock.
A thong bathing suit for men.

given instructions about condoms using bananas for classroom demonstrations. The best-selling vibrator in Germany resembles a banana. And you can forget the sex therapist: bananas are rich in B vitamins, which are believed to help produce sex hormones.

"Being a sex symbol is a heavy load to carry," Marilyn Monroe once complained. So just imagine the burden on a Banana Split. Our fondness for the theatrical dessert moves beyond its suggestive banana to include immodest breast-shaped scoops of ice cream, dripping with warm syrups, bathed in sweet sauces, primped with frothy whipped cream, and dolled-up with a lipstick-red cherry. The voluptuous Banana Split is as obvious as Ms. Monroe in a tight dress.

In the 1970s, Blums Ice Cream Parlor at Polk and California Streets in San Francisco provided a genteel setting for dainty sandwiches and heavenly coffee cake. Blums's most popular dish, however, was the Banana Split (intended for sharing, of course). One banana was split to form the base of the ice cream, and a second banana was cut into quarters and placed at the ends of the dish. A large scoop of chocolate ice cream was mounted over scoops of vanilla and strawberry. The dessert was topped with hot fudge, crushed strawberries, and marshmallow crème, and decorated with whipped cream from a pastry bag with a number-6 decorating tip. Price: $1.85.

THE BANANA AS IT RIPENS

1-PARTIALLY RIPE BANANA yellow with green tip—
In this state bananas should be cooked and eaten as a vegetable.

2-YELLOW RIPE BANANA without trace of green—
The fruit now has a delicious flavor and is readily digested.

3-FULLY RIPE BANANA flecked with brown—Now at its best for flavor
and nutrition and of all foods one of the most easily digested.

Chapter 5

Civilized Gluttony

Moderation is a fatal thing. Nothing succeeds like excess.

— Oscar Wilde

Americans have never bought into the theory that less is more. Big has always been better here, as the folks in Selinsgrove, Pennsylvania, can attest. Their town has held the undisputed Banana Split World Record ever since April 30, 1988, when fundraisers assembled a dessert measuring 4.55 miles in length along Market Street. The Selinsgrove High School Band sponsored the event as its main fundraiser that year, and volunteers engineered the construction of the longest continuous dish ever to hold a Banana Split. The previous record was for a construct of bananas and ice cream that measured a mere 1.33 miles.

The band enlisted a cardboard manufacturer to produce a thick corrugated cylinder that served as the Banana Split container. The cylinder "dish" was opened up, supported on sawhorses, then lined with aluminum foil. Band members obtained approval

> **Backfield in Potion**
>
> The South Bend Chocolate Café salutes its neighbor, the College Football Hall of Fame, with a four-scoop Banana Split called The Four Horsemen, inspired by Notre Dame's fabled backfield.

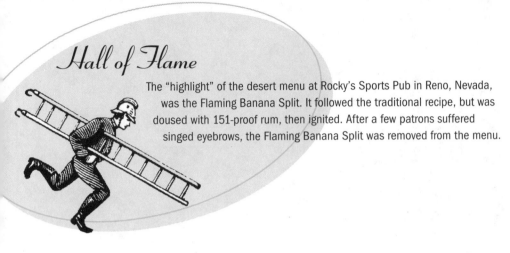

Hall of Flame

The "highlight" of the desert menu at Rocky's Sports Pub in Reno, Nevada, was the Flaming Banana Split. It followed the traditional recipe, but was doused with 151-proof rum, then ignited. After a few patrons suffered singed eyebrows, the Flaming Banana Split was removed from the menu.

from the town council to block off the downtown street for four hours, allowing enough time to set up, serve, eat, and clean up the mess.

Tickets were numbered from 0001 to 8000, with each number corresponding to the number on a section of the dish, and captains were put in charge of 25-foot stretches of the lengthy dessert. They received written instructions telling them what to do when, and each was given a box containing 25 bananas, foil, a rubbish bag, toppings for the ice cream, and ice cream scoops. Captains directed ticket holders within their designated areas.

At a predetermined time, an ice cream truck drove down the closed-off street, making deliveries to each section of the "dish," as everyone prepared to assemble the ingredients. Then a local radio station issued orders over the air for each procedure. Finally, the station announced that the entire Banana Split had been completed, and the crowd of 8,000 began eating.

With the ticket price set at $2 each, the high school band realized a tidy profit of $10,000. And, of course, 4.55 miles was good enough for recognition

Ice Cream Castles in the Air

With an operating merry-go-round in front plus house-made ice cream, puppets, trains, and flying mechanical toy wonders within, Ella's Deli is a Madison, Wisconsin, institution and every hometown kid's fantasy destination for dessert. It was opened in 1963 by Ella Hirschfeld, who created a Banana Split called The Kazoo: 32 scoops of ice cream, 5 bananas, blueberries, strawberries, pineapple, cherries, and one entire can of whipped cream.

Field of Dreams

At the end of every fall season, the University of Georgia's baseball team divides into two squads and plays a seven-game series. At stake: Banana Splits that members of the losing team must make for members of the winning team after the squad's deciding contest. Three scoops and you're out!

Jumbo Banana Split

Boogie's Diner, Aspen, Colorado

Split 1 banana lengthwise and place the halves parallel on a Banana Split dish. Ladle 2 ounces each of hot fudge and caramel syrup over the banana. Place 1 scoop each of vanilla, chocolate, and strawberry ice cream between the banana halves. Garnish with whipped cream, and sprinkle with pecans and walnuts. Drizzle with chocolate, strawberry, and caramel syrups, and place a whole cherry at the top.

Pig's Dinner Sundae

Sherman's Dairy Bar, South Haven, Michigan

Line a wooden container shaped like a pig's trough with waxed paper. Split 1 large banana lengthwise, and place the halves on the bottom of the container. Place 1 scoop each of vanilla, chocolate, strawberry, and butter pecan ice cream between the banana halves. Spoon 2 ounces each of chocolate syrup, marshmallow creme, crushed strawberries, and crushed pineapple over the scoops of ice cream. Garnish with whipped cream, sprinkle with chopped mixed nuts, and place 5 whole cherries at the top. (If you are dining at Sherman's Dairy Bar and you finish the entire Split, you receive a button that reads "I made a pig of myself at Sherman's."

Super 4-Way Banana Split

Schneider's Restaurant, Avon-by-the-Sea, New Jersey

Split 1 banana lengthwise and place the halves parallel on a Banana Split dish. Place 1 scoop each of vanilla, chocolate, coffee, and "meat loaf" ice cream between the banana halves. Ladle 2 ounces each of hot fudge and hot caramel syrup over the ice cream. Garnish with whipped cream, sprinkle with dark chocolate chips and chopped walnuts, and serve with a chocolate-chip cookie.

BANANA ROYAL

SERVICE	INGREDIENTS	PORTIONS
Banana Royal Dish	Banana	1 whole
7¼" Underliner	Vanilla Ice Cream	#20 scoop, with lip
Teaspoon	Strawberry Ice Cream	#20 scoop, with lip
	Pineapple Fruit	1 ounce
	Strawberry Fruit	1 ounce
	Whipped Cream	1 ounce band
	Chopped Nuts	1 teaspoon
	Cherry	1 whole

1. Trim ends of banana.

2. Cut unpeeled banana in half, lengthwise, being careful not to break banana.

3. Place both peeled halves in dish with cut surface down and ends pointed outward.

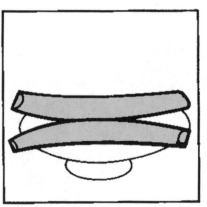

4. Place one #20 scoop of vanilla ice cream and one #20 scoop of strawberry ice cream in a straight line on top of the banana halves.

5. Ladle one ounce of pineapple fruit over the vanilla ice cream.

6. Ladle one ounce of strawberry fruit over the strawberry ice cream.

7. Dispense band of whipped cream between the two scoops of ice cream.

8. Sprinkle one teaspoon of chopped nuts over all.

9. Garnish with a cherry.

Quad-City Special

Lagomarcino's, Moline, Illinois

Split 1 banana lengthwise and place the halves parallel on a Banana Split dish. Place 2 scoops of vanilla ice cream between the banana halves. Ladle 2 ounces of cherry topping over one scoop and 2 ounces of crushed pineapple over the other. Garnish with whipped cream, sprinkle with chopped mixed nuts, and place a whole cherry at the top. On either side of the scoops of ice cream place Oreo cookies to represent paddlewheels.

Banana Split Schooner

Landmark Restaurant, Williamsburg, Iowa

Line the bottom of a large footed glass schooner with soft-serve vanilla ice cream. Split 1 banana lengthwise and place the halves parallel over the ice cream. Place 3 tall swirls of soft-serve vanilla ice cream between the banana halves, and ladle 2 ounces of each of 3 toppings of your choice over the ice cream. Garnish with whipped cream, sprinkle with chopped mixed nuts, and place 3 whole cherries at the top.

Papa Bear Banana Split

Mammoth Lakes Ice Creamery, Mammoth Lakes, California

Place a warm marshmallow-fudge brownie at the bottom of a large oval bowl. Split 1 banana lengthwise and place the halves parallel over the brownie. Place 5 scoops of ice cream (your choice of flavors) between the banana halves, and ladle 2 ounces of each of 3 toppings of your choice over the ice cream. Garnish with whipped cream, sprinkle with chopped mixed nuts, and place 5 whole cherries at the top.

Key Words

Brûlée. French word meaning "burnt." Banana halves can be sprinkled with sugar and placed under a broiler or heated with a handheld butane torch until the sugar melts and caramelizes. The banana has been brûléed.

Monkey Love Banana Split

Baleen, Coconut Grove, Florida

Layer the bottom of a hardened pastry shell with 2 ounces each of chocolate and caramel syrups (follow the directions on a store-bought pastry shell; use a bowl to shape the pastry before baking). Place 1 small scoop each of hazelnut, coffee, vanilla, and chocolate ice cream in the shell. Slice 1 banana into disks, sprinkle them with sugar, heat them with a small butane blowtorch or under a broiler until the sugar melts and caramelizes (see sidebar), and arrange them around the scoops of ice cream. Spoon fresh diced pineapple, diced mangos, and mixed fresh berries over the ice cream, garnish with whipped cream, and sprinkle with candied walnuts.

by the *Guinness Book of World Records* as the longest Banana Split ever made.

Measuring food in miles is a symptom of cultural excess, according to at least one culinary critic. Damon Lee Fowler, writing in *Southern Voice*, employed the term *Banana Split Personality Disorder* to describe our nation's pervasive bigger-is-better mentality and our obsession with supersizing practically everything we eat. He concludes that our portion sizes have grown, in some cases, to double or triple their original size.

"But a classic Banana Split is supposed to be big," replies Jim Powers. Jim and his wife Patricia Kelly Powers are the proprietors of an Ocean City, Maryland, institution called Kelly's Front Porch, nationally known for Banana Splits of jaw-dropping proportions.

A midlife crisis lured Powers away from an insurance brokerage in Elmira,

> **There was just too much of it. . . . It was like having a Banana Split with every meal.**
>
> — Russell Baker, explaining why he stopped being a sports fan

Key Words

Calories. In his novelty song "Banana Split for My Baby," Louis Prima croons, "Dispenser man, if you please, serve my chick a mess of calories." A medium-size banana contains about 100 calories; a traditional Banana Split may easily spiral over 1,000 calories.

Go Hog Wild Banana Split

Barbeque Center, Lexington, North Carolina

Split 1 banana lengthwise and place the halves parallel on a Banana Split dish. Place 1 scoop each of vanilla, chocolate, and strawberry ice cream between the banana halves. Ladle 2 ounces of chocolate syrup and 2 ounces of maple syrup with crushed walnuts over all. Garnish with whipped cream, and place 3 whole cherries at the top.

Riverboat Paddlewheel

Betty Jane's Candies, Dubuque, Iowa

Split 1 banana lengthwise and place the halves parallel on a Banana Split dish. Place 1 scoop each of vanilla, chocolate, and strawberry ice cream between the banana halves. Ladle 2 ounces of crushed pineapple over the vanilla, 2 ounces of chocolate syrup over the chocolate, and 2 ounces of strawberry topping over the strawberry ice cream. On either side of the scoops of ice cream place Oreo cookies to represent paddlewheels; between the scoops of ice cream place sugar wafers; into the top stick a pirouette cookie to represent a smokestack. Garnish with swirls of whipped cream, and sprinkle with chopped mixed nuts and chocolate sprinkles.

Son of Frankenstein

Zephyr Café, Chicago, Illinois

Place 1 scoop each of vanilla, chocolate, and strawberry ice cream in a row on a Banana Split dish. Split 1 banana lengthwise and press the halves against either side of the ice cream. Ladle 2 ounces of crushed pineapple over the vanilla, 2 ounces of chocolate syrup over the chocolate, and 2 ounces of sliced, fresh strawberries over the strawberry ice cream. Garnish with whipped cream, sprinkle with sliced almonds, and place a whole cherry at the top. Add a pirouette cookie on the side.

How to Eat a Banana Split

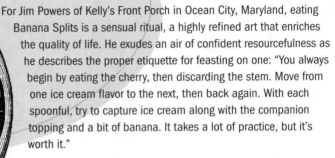

For Jim Powers of Kelly's Front Porch in Ocean City, Maryland, eating Banana Splits is a sensual ritual, a highly refined art that enriches the quality of life. He exudes an air of confident resourcefulness as he describes the proper etiquette for feasting on one: "You always begin by eating the cherry, then discarding the stem. Move from one ice cream flavor to the next, then back again. With each spoonful, try to capture ice cream along with the companion topping and a bit of banana. It takes a lot of practice, but it's worth it."

" **The lady created a Banana Split of devastating proportions, almost crippling two young boys who attempted to eat one between them. A Banana Split such as this was built upon a solid foundation of impenetrable chocolate cake. It sat firmly upon a large oval plate, and included the usual peanuts and ice cream. The banana itself was drowned and lost in the creation somewhere. Raspberry sauce signified its grisly demise. "**

— **From the short story *"The Lady from the Lake Rabun Hotel,"* by Richard Hayward**

Stock Split

If a New Yorker thinks he is eating the best of something, he will practically beg you to take his wallet. Legendary impresario Warner Leroy provided undisputed proof. For many years, the menu at Tavern on the Green, his restaurant in New York's Central Park, spotlighted the most expensive (at $10) Banana Split in America, with macadamia-vanilla, chocolate, and strawberry ice cream, raspberry, butterscotch, and hot fudge toppings, brownie chunks, whipped cream, sprinkles, and nuts.

Big Pink Banana Split

The Big Pink, Miami Beach, Florida

Split 1 banana lengthwise and place the halves parallel on a Banana Split dish. Place 1 scoop each of vanilla, chocolate, and strawberry ice cream between the banana halves. Ladle 2 ounces of crushed pineapple over the vanilla, 2 ounces of hot fudge over the chocolate, and 2 ounces of crushed strawberries over the strawberry ice cream. Garnish with "pink" whipped cream (tinted with food coloring), sprinkle with chopped walnuts, and place a whole cherry at the top.

Oregon Split

Zinger's, Seaside, Oregon

Split 1 banana lengthwise and place the halves parallel on a Banana Split dish. Place 1 scoop each of vanilla, chocolate, and strawberry ice cream between the banana halves. Ladle 2 ounces of crushed pineapple over the vanilla, 2 ounces of chocolate syrup over the chocolate, and 2 ounces of blackberry sauce over the strawberry. Garnish with whipped cream, and place a whole cherry at the top.

Madonna's Delight

Madonna Inn, San Luis Obispo, California

Split 1 banana lengthwise, then cut the split halves again widthwise. Place the banana spears around the edges of a large glass goblet. Place 1 scoop each of vanilla, chocolate, and strawberry ice cream, one on top of another, in the goblet. Ladle 2 ounces of caramel syrup and 2 ounces of mocha fudge topping over all. Garnish with whipped cream, sprinkle with toasted almonds, and place a whole cherry at the top.

Bear Market

Boyds Bear Country is a retail and corporate office building located five miles south of historic Gettysburg, Pennsylvania, the flagship store for the Boyds Bear Collection. The store resembles a southern Pennsylvania-style bank barn and features an operating restaurant with one doozer of a Banana Split on the menu.

Order a Tu-Tu-Much Sundae and you get a 30-ounce bowl with a warm brownie on the bottom, six scoops of ice cream, two bananas sliced into disks, and your choice of toppings, nuts, and sprinkles. It's covered with whipped cream, then decorated with gummy bears. If you eat it all, you get a free Ballerina Bear wearing an apron that reads "I Ate Tu-Tu-Much at Boyds."

New York, in 1989 to the helm of the only ice cream parlor on the Ocean City boardwalk. There, in a neighborhood of arcades, minigolf courses, and roller coasters, he has re-created, in his words, "the ambience and attitude of the soda fountains of my youth." He contends that the Banana Split has always taken center stage in classic fountains, so he has built the reputation of Kelly's on a throwback to the noble dessert, one certainly not intended for the weight-conscious.

Someone once said, "If you can't make it good, make it big." Kelly's makes it good *and* big. For better or for worse, Kelly's offers the Hall of Fame Banana Split, a pyramid-shaped behemoth served in an oversize bowl. Four scoops of ice cream are placed at the bottom, then bathed in syrups. Next, three more scoops of ice cream are placed on top, and smothered with cookies, candies, and crushed peanuts. Two whole bananas are split lengthwise, cut in half again, mounted vertically around

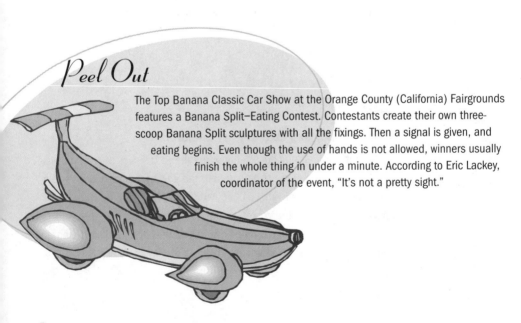

Peel Out

The Top Banana Classic Car Show at the Orange County (California) Fairgrounds features a Banana Split–Eating Contest. Contestants create their own three-scoop Banana Split sculptures with all the fixings. Then a signal is given, and eating begins. Even though the use of hands is not allowed, winners usually finish the whole thing in under a minute. According to Eric Lackey, coordinator of the event, "It's not a pretty sight."

Three-Scoop Banana Split

Blossom Deli & Soda Fountain, Charleston, West Virginia

Split 1 banana lengthwise and place the halves parallel on a Banana Split dish. Place 1 scoop each of vanilla, chocolate, and strawberry ice cream between the banana halves. Ladle 2 ounces of crushed pineapple over the vanilla, 2 ounces of hot fudge over the chocolate, and 2 ounces of strawberry topping over the strawberry ice cream. Drizzle caramel syrup over all. Garnish each scoop of ice cream with an individual swirl of whipped cream, and place a whole cherry at the top of each peak. Sprinkle with chopped mixed nuts, if desired.

World's Best Banana Split

The Creamery, Sevierville, Tennessee

Split 1 banana lengthwise and place the halves parallel on a Banana Split dish. Place 1 scoop each of French Vanilla Bean, Caramel Turtle, and Smokey Mountain Fudge ice cream between the banana halves. Ladle 2 ounces of crushed pineapple over the French Vanilla Bean, 2 ounces of hot caramel over the Caramel Turtle, and 2 ounces of hot fudge over the Smokey Mountain Fudge ice cream. Garnish with whipped cream, sprinkle with pecan pieces, and place 3 whole cherries at the top.

The Be-Here-Now'm Banana Split

Grateful Bean Café, Oklahoma City, Oklahoma

Split 1 banana lengthwise and place the halves parallel on a Banana Split dish. Place 1 scoop each of vanilla, chocolate, and strawberry ice cream between the banana halves. Spoon 2 ounces of chocolate syrup over the vanilla, 2 ounces of marshmallow creme over the chocolate, and 2 ounces of strawberry topping over the strawberry ice cream. Garnish with whipped cream, sprinkle with freshly roasted pistachios, and place 3 whole cherries at the top.

Jungle Warfare

When Captain Lorenzo Baker arrived in the port of Boston with his first shipment of bananas, his Cape Cod neighbors derided the fruit as "monkey food." As a result of their craving for bananas, combined with their skill in removing the fruit from the trees, monkeys account for millions of dollars in revenues lost by plantations every year.

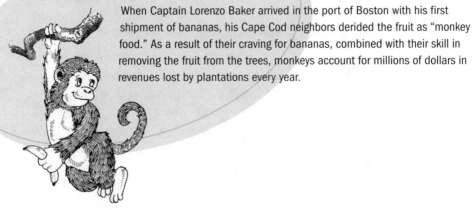

❝ The Banana Split is the most outlandish and flamboyant dairy preparation of all. . . . Whoever orders one of these mountainous concoctions seems to be undertaking a feat like defying gravity or scaling Mt. Everest. But spoonful by heaping spoonful, cherries, nuts, whipped cream, ice cream and banana gradually disappear. And when it is finished, a look of triumph spreads over the snacker's face, and it is clear that he feels superior to other mortals for this accomplishment. ❞

— From an article by Dale Brown that appeared in *Holiday* magazine

Weigh-in

Hawaiian-born sumo wrestling legend Akebono tips the scales at 530 pounds on a diet that borders on force-feeding. When he opened a restaurant in Akasaka, Japan, his dessert menu featured a larger-than-life upright Banana Split served in a glass mug.

Monkey Business

Ice Cream Corner, North Clearwater, Florida

Split 1 banana lengthwise and place the halves parallel on a Banana Split dish. Place 2 scoops of vanilla ice cream between the banana halves. Ladle 2 ounces of hot fudge over one scoop and 2 ounces of hot caramel over the other. Garnish with whipped cream, and place a whole cherry at the top.

Monkey in the Middle Sundae

A. K. Diamond's, Nantucket, Massachusetts

Place a warm brownie at the center of a round dish, and top with 2 scoops of vanilla ice cream. Ladle 2 ounces of caramel syrup over one scoop and 2 ounces of chocolate syrup over the other. Split 1 banana lengthwise and press the halves against either side of the ice cream. Garnish with whipped cream, sprinkle with pieces of Heath Bar, and place a whole cherry at the top.

King Kong Banana Split

Young's Jersey Dairy, Yellow Springs, Ohio

Split 1 banana lengthwise and place the halves on the bottom of a "foot-long" Banana Split dish. Place 1 scoop each of vanilla, chocolate, and strawberry ice cream between the banana halves. This is the first layer of ice cream. On top of the first ice cream layer, place 1 scoop of vanilla ice cream and 1 scoop of chocolate ice cream. Ladle 2 ounces each of chocolate syrup, crushed pineapple, and crushed strawberries over all. Garnish with whipped cream, sprinkle with chopped peanuts, and place 2 animal crackers and a whole cherry at the top.

TRAVEL REALLY "BROADENS" ONE!

> ❝ I'll bet you the biggest Banana Split you can find that no one will guess that we've switched identities. ❞
>
> — From *The Banana Split Affair* by Cynthia Blair

> ❝ Banana Splits for breakfast. I think I ate about five. ❞
>
> — Sissy Spacek as Babe in the film *Crimes of the Heart*

Split Level

From a quaint restaurant at the summit of Hong Kong's Victoria Peak, you can have dinner far above the city lights below. For dessert, the Peak Café Banana Split includes vanilla, chocolate, and strawberry ice cream, covered with chocolate syrup and topped with fresh blueberries, mango, strawberries, and a "peak" of whipped cream.

the heap of ice cream, then covered with a lavish blanket of whipped cream and decorated with a fistful of cherries.

"It comes with a pair of stretch pants," jokes Powers. His customers are allowed to pick and choose which flavors of ice cream go where, and in what order the toppings are applied. There are sometimes heated discussions when the dessert is being assembled for communal sharing, since the Hall of Fame Banana Split can feed as many as 10 people, all of whom have individual preferences.

Customers root for brave comrades who attempt to devour the whole caboodle single-handedly. If you do so, you get your picture posted and your name inscribed on the "Wall of Fame." It's a distinct badge of honor for Luther Murphy, Jr., or "Pennsylvania Pete," as

Tropico Kong

Silver Spurs, New York, New York

Split 1 banana lengthwise and place the halves parallel on a Banana Split dish. Place 1 scoop each of vanilla, chocolate, and strawberry ice cream between the banana halves. Ladle 3 ounces of chocolate syrup over all. Garnish each scoop of ice cream with an individual swirl of whipped cream, sprinkle with walnuts, and place a whole cherry at the top of each peak.

Drunken Monkey

Earth and Ocean Restaurant, Seattle Washington

Split 1 unpeeled banana lengthwise, and marinate the halves overnight in Myer's dark rum (enough to cover the banana halves), a squeeze of fresh lime juice, and a pinch of brown sugar. Peel the banana halves and grill them in a panini iron. Arrange the grilled banana halves on a round platter with 1 scoop each of chocolate and coconut sorbet, and decorate with red tuiles (thin, crisp, curled cookies).

Gorilla's Treat

Dumser's Dairyland Drive-in, Ocean City, Maryland

Split 1 banana lengthwise and place the halves parallel on a Banana Split dish. Place 3 scoops of banana ice cream between the banana halves. Ladle 3 ounces of chocolate syrup over all. Garnish with whipped cream, and place a whole cherry at the top.

Hot Zone Banana Split

Chino Latino, Minneapolis, Minnesota

Split 4 bananas lengthwise and arrange all of the slices parallel to each other on a 14-inch round platter. Over the bananas place 4 scoops each of vanilla and coconut ice cream. Ladle 3 ounces of caramel sauce, 3 ounces of chocolate syrup, and 3 ounces of rum-spiked crushed pineapple over all. Garnish with a tall portion of whipped cream, sprinkle with toasted coconut and macadamia nuts, and decorate with small plastic monkeys, donkeys, and bulls (usually used to decorate beverages).

Wonder of the World

Their Indian heritage was a compelling influence when Bharatkumar and Rohini Joshi turned an old-fashioned pharmacy into an ice cream parlor in Bethlehem, Pennsylvania, in 1989. In fact, they named a six-scoop Banana Split after India's architectural wonder, the Taj Mahal. While you may choose familiar flavors for your own Taj Mahal, the more adventurous patrons of Nuts About Ice Cream select from such exotic ice cream offerings as saffron, fig, mango, honey-lavender, sesame-tahini, vanilla-hulva, and sapota. Toppings are house-made and inspired by seasonal fruits, and rich whipped cream is crowned with special "jumbo" cherries.

> **A Banana Split is too big for a kid. It's something you've got to grow into.**
>
> — **Lisa Rose-Adams, co-owner of a Las Vegas Dairy Queen, on why adults purchase most Banana Splits**

> **I eat really well, but when I want to have a Banana Split, I have it.**
>
> — **Shania Twain**

Bon Vivant

It's not hard to imagine Steven Bruce, the impresario of Serendipity 3, as the hero of a novel. Suave and sporting a Hercule Poirot mustache, he carries himself with the aura of a statesman, or, perhaps, a university president. He dressed windows at Macy's before dreaming up the campy sundaes at this New York City institution. For the past 50 years he has satisfied the sweet teeth of people like Cary Grant, Grace Kelly, Marilyn Monroe, and Jackie Kennedy with exaggerated notions like the five-scoop Outrageous Banana Split. In addition to the regular-size Split, the menu offers a "Coward's Portion" (three scoops), which, politely said, is what you order if you're on a diet.

Eat at Your Own Risk

The 5 Spot restaurant in Seattle is the home of a Banana Split known as "The Bulge." It's a banana, battered, rolled in sugar, deep-fried, and served with ice cream, whipped cream, and macadamia nuts. But there's a catch. Before diners give in to self-indulgence, they are required to sign a waiver that reads as follows:

I, _____, release 5 Spot from all liability of any weight gain that may result from ordering and devouring this sinfully fattening treat. I will not impose any sort of "Obesity-Related" lawsuit against 5 Spot or consider any similar type of frivolous legislation created by a hungry trial lawyer.

5 Spot will not be held liable in any way if the result of my eating this dessert leads to a "Spare Tire," "Love Handles," "Saddle Bags," or "Junk in My Trunk." If I have to go to "Fat Camp" at some time in my life, I will not mail my bill to 5 Spot.

I knowingly and willingly accept full and personal responsibility for my choices and actions.

Lock, Stock, and Wheelbarrow

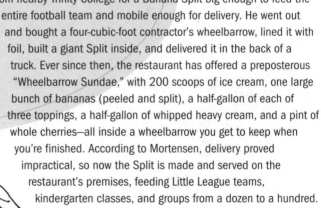

Twenty years ago, ice cream entrepreneur Rodney Mortensen of Mortensen's in Newington, Connecticut, got an order from nearby Trinity College for a Banana Split big enough to feed the entire football team and mobile enough for delivery. He went out and bought a four-cubic-foot contractor's wheelbarrow, lined it with foil, built a giant Split inside, and delivered it in the back of a truck. Ever since then, the restaurant has offered a preposterous "Wheelbarrow Sundae," with 200 scoops of ice cream, one large bunch of bananas (peeled and split), a half-gallon of each of three toppings, a half-gallon of whipped heavy cream, and a pint of whole cherries—all inside a wheelbarrow you get to keep when you're finished. According to Mortensen, delivery proved impractical, so now the Split is made and served on the restaurant's premises, feeding Little League teams, kindergarten classes, and groups from a dozen to a hundred.

> **Why, I've known some bananafish to swim into a banana hole and eat as many as seventy-eight bananas.**
>
> — From *A Perfect Day for Bananafish* by J. D. Salinger

he's known at Kelly's. Retired from his job at the chocolate factory in Hershey, he regularly makes the three-hour drive from his home in Mechanicsburg, Pennsylvania, drawn to Ocean City by the seductive song of the "whale" of a Banana Split. In 2002, Murphy ate the season's first Hall of Fame Banana Split in March, the season's last Split on Thanksgiving weekend, and nine more Hall of Fame Banana Splits in between.

Americans are a competitive sort, as competitive about eating as they are about sports, so it's not surprising that a Banana Split challenge was born at Kelly's. As it turns out, however, a more popular choice is still Kelly's Olde Fashioned Banana Split, a more traditional (and less extreme) triple-scoop serving for patrons whom Powers refers to as "Hofits"—Hall of Famers in Training.

Powers has found in Ocean City an ideal vantage point for dishing up the Banana Split in its full glory. Most of his customers are there on vacation, so rules and regulations—especially about

Walking Tall

The high-reaching pastry crew of Atlanta's Hi Life Kitchen produces a visual and gastronomic spectacle called the Fried Banana Split. Halves of a split banana are individually wrapped in phyllo dough, rolled in toasted pecans and walnuts, then deep-fried. The fried bananas are put in a boat-shaped dish, ice cream and toppings are added, a huge phyllo sail is erected—rising a foot into the air—and the dessert is ready to sail into the dining room.

Splitting Up

Created by grocery-chain mogul Michael Bonfante of Nob Hill Foods, Bonfante Gardens is a combination horticultural theme park and amusement park set among 75 acres of countryside in Gilroy, California. Visitors can check out the "Circus Trees" transplanted from the Santa Cruz mountains, then enjoy such food-themed rides as the Garlic Twirl, the Mushroom Swing, the Artichoke Dip, or the belly-turning Banana Split—a banana-shaped boat that swings back and forth ever higher and ever faster.

If the Shoe Fits …

The Glass Slipper Banana Split is a fairy tale of a dessert. In fact, if Cinderella were alive today, you could almost imagine her sharing this ridiculously rich dessert with Prince Charming at Cinderella's Café in Sylvan Beach, New York. A huge glass bowl (slipper) is filled with a split banana and 12 scoops of ice cream smothered with half a dozen toppings. If you finish every bite, you're rewarded with a sparkling Cinderella crown and a roll of Tums.

" A crawfish is like a Banana Split is to you and me. It's what they're after. "

— Mark Rose, on the bait he used to catch an award-winning bass

" To create the menu wording for a Banana Split Sundae, you might print 'Half the Calories' set large and bold above a photo of the Sundae. Then, below those words, in parentheses, is the statement 'When You Share One with a Friend!' "

— Michael J. Motto, on how to advertise

Mother of All Banana Splits

A giant Banana Split was the "Flagship of Farrell's Fleet of Fabulous Fountain Fantasies." The now-defunct old-fashioned ice cream parlors, fathered by Bob Farrell in 1963, served a dessert that featured three scoops of extra-rich vanilla, chocolate, and strawberry ice cream nesting on a split banana, smothered with pineapple, strawberry topping, and Holland Dutch chocolate, then crowned with gobs of real whipped cream and topped with nuts, a ruby-red cherry, and an American flag. For expectant mothers, the Banana Split was served with "a split dill pickle upon request."

Fountain of Youth

After school, giggling teenagers crowd into the Lyons Soda Fountain, in Lyons, Colorado, just as they have since 1921. Banana Splits, it seems, have never gone out of style there, and it's useless, at this late date, to ask the kids to show restraint. Soda jerks still assemble a whopping Banana Split they call the Lyons Roar, with 3 bananas, 10 scoops of ice cream, hot fudge, hot butterscotch, marshmallow topping, whipped cream, peanuts, and half a dozen cherries. Youth, after all, must be served.

eating—are left at home. "They've come to splurge," says Powers. Although it may seem strange, if not nervy, that in the midst of America's battle against too-muchness, a place like Kelly's so openly celebrates overeating, Powers's motive for expanding the dimensions of his Split is, of course, skillful marketing. Big is dramatic. Big is thrilling. Big sells.

Some might consider the jumbo Banana Split dreamed up by the folks at Kelly's to be gluttonous. They should be enlightened by the words of a pleasingly plump 19th-century author named Elizabeth Robbins Pennell, who wrote: "Gluttony is ranked with the deadly sins; it should be honored with the cardinal virtues."

" The Banana Republic chain is going to open stores catering to plus-sized people. They're going to call it Banana Split Republic. "

— Jay Leno

Plumbing the Depths

Everything but the kitchen sink—that's what goes into the screwball Banana Split at Jaxson's Ice Cream Parlor in Dania Beach, Florida. It starts with a stainless-steel hotel pan supported by a wooden base and attached plumbing, so it even looks like a kitchen sink. A minimum of four customers each choose three flavors of ice cream for assembly in the "sink." The ice cream is flooded with chocolate syrup, cherry-pineapple topping, crushed strawberries, and marshmallow creme, surrounded with split bananas, showered with whipped cream, and sprinkled with nuts. Burning sparklers add pyrotechnics, and the wail of a fire-truck siren announces the delivery of each Kitchen Sink.

Climb Every Mountain

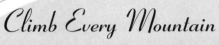

Abundance is the theme at The Mountaineer, an eatery in Church Hill, Tennessee. The Mountaineer Banana Split is an architectural feat, built around nine scoops of ice cream, and dished up by owners N. E. and Betty Moore. Waiters carry the creations to the table slowly, and in both hands, so the four-inch-high covering of whipped cream won't slide off.

Pin Split

Tenpins

In bowling alley lingo, when your 1, 2, 3, 4, and 7 pins are left in the rack, it's called a Banana Split.

Some Like It Hot

Turn a mug of hot cocoa into a Banana Split Hot Cocoa. Place $2\frac{1}{2}$ cups milk, $\frac{1}{2}$ cup cocoa powder, $\frac{1}{2}$ cup sugar, one-quarter of a banana (sliced), and 1 tablespoon of strawberry jam in a blender, and mix until smooth. Pour the mixture into a saucepan, and stir over medium heat until hot. Pour into a mug, top with whipped cream, drizzle with chocolate syrup, sprinkle with nuts, and place a whole cherry at the top.

Chapter 6

Top Banana

> **All passions exaggerate; and they are passions only because they do exaggerate.**
>
> — Sébastien-Roch Nicolas de Chamfort

He goes bananas over bananas. Ken Bannister, a public relations guru and longtime scholar of banana consciousness, shampoos his hair with mashed bananas, polishes his shoes with banana peels, and eats a Banana Split every night before bedtime. Since 1972 he has been the self-appointed Grand Pooh-Bah of the International Banana Club, now numbering nearly 10,000 members who refer to him as "Top Banana." Not coincidently, he serves as curator of the Banana Museum in Altadena, California, where he has assembled 17,000 banana-shaped, banana-flavored, and banana-themed artifacts. They include the treasured photograph of himself with Jay Leno on *The Tonight Show*, hanging next to a framed and mounted petrified banana.

Perhaps because it is so universal and commonplace, the banana doesn't

Split Parade

It was arguably the most popular song of the 1920s. Legend has it that songwriters Frank Silver and Irving Cohn overheard a Greek fruit peddler utter the memorable words "Yes, we have no bananas." Their novelty song was introduced by Eddie Cantor on the vaudeville stage, and the rest is history. Unlike most popular songs of the era, it never faded in popularity and even today it's one of the few 80-year-old songs that practically everyone has heard.

stir this kind of passion in most people. But then, Ken Bannister isn't "most people." He is a tireless motivational speaker and marketing executive who embraced an attention-getting device that was ripe for the picking. "You must get your audience's attention and recognition if you're trying to sell something," insists Bannister, a man of interesting, engaging eccentricities.

It is difficult to separate Bannister from the banana. All of his work is driven by what he calls "the meal in a peel." Whimsically attired in a bright yellow blazer with the cartoon logo of his International Banana Club sewn into the right lapel, he greets his audiences by asking, "Do you want to see a Banana Split?" He then pulls a banana from his pocket and snaps it in two. It's his calling card. But he has a hard time knowing when to stop. "For what, after all, is a banana," Bannister asks, "but a yellow smile?" He seems to possess the unshakable, upbeat attitude of a cheerleader.

Split the Vote

Inspired by the 1948 presidential campaign, early TV's Howdy Doody decided to run for "President of All the Boys and Girls." Howdy's platform promised: "Cut-rate Banana Splits, two Christmas holidays, only one school day each year, double sodas for a dime, plenty of movies, more pictures in history books, plus free circus and rodeo admissions." Based on a tally of Wonder Bread labels mailed to the show, Howdy won the election.

Banana Fo-Fana Split

Dolphin Fountain, Lake Buena Vista, Florida

Split 1 banana lengthwise and place the halves parallel on a Banana Split dish. Place 1 scoop each of vanilla, chocolate, and strawberry ice cream between the banana halves. Ladle 2 ounces of crushed pineapple over the vanilla, 2 ounces of hot fudge over the chocolate, and 2 ounces of strawberry topping over the strawberry ice cream. Garnish with whipped cream, sprinkle with salted peanuts, and place a whole cherry at the top.

Nanana Bo-nanana

Rosie's Diner, Monument, Colorado

Split 1 banana lengthwise and place the halves parallel on a Banana Split dish. Place 1 scoop each of vanilla, chocolate, and strawberry ice cream between the banana halves. Ladle 2 ounces of crushed pineapple and 2 ounces of strawberry topping over all. Garnish with whipped cream, and ladle 2 ounces of wet walnuts (see sidebar on page 28) over the top.

Ben and Jerry's Revolt

Kiss, Miami Beach, Florida

Place a white-chocolate brownie in the center of a round platter and top it with 2 scoops of Ben & Jerry's Chunky Monkey ice cream. Ladle 2 ounces of chocolate syrup over one scoop and 2 ounces of caramel syrup over the other. Split 1 banana lengthwise and press the halves against either side of the ice cream. Garnish with whipped cream, and sprinkle with small pieces of pecan brittle.

No Pain, No Gain

The sport of wrestling provides a move called the "Banana Split." If your opponent has turtled and you are on his side, wrap your legs around his near knee. Grab his far bent leg around his calf and thigh and pull it toward your chest, putting pressure on his hips. Keep pulling and fall back until his rear end is on your stomach. Then pull back with your arms, pull down with your legs, and push up with your hips. Your opponent's hips will be in a world of pain.

> **Life is just a bowl of cherries? Nah, life is a Banana Split.**
>
> — **Ken Bannister, "Top Banana" of the International Banana Club**

> **I should've really kept track of how many Banana Splits it takes to cross the country.**
>
> — **Todd Mills on his 5,052-mile bicycle journey from the East Coast to the West Coast during the summer of 2001**

Guilty Pleasure

Before he was executed by the State of Oklahoma for a 1985 murder, Randall Eugene Cannon ate his last meal—a 21-piece shrimp dinner, a five-piece fish dinner, a Dr Pepper, and a Banana Split.

Harem Sharem'm

Green Gables, Sioux City, Iowa

Split 1 banana lengthwise and place the halves parallel on a Banana Split dish. Place 1 scoop of chocolate ice cream between the banana halves. On each side of the chocolate place 1 scoop of vanilla ice cream. Ladle 3 ounces of chocolate syrup over all. Garnish between the scoops of ice cream with whipped cream, sprinkle with lightly salted toasted almonds, and place half a cherry at the top of each whipped-cream peak. Soak 2 sugar cubes in pure lemon extract, place them on the cherries, and carefully light them with a long match just prior to serving.

Krispy-Kreme Banana Split

Vista Riverside Grille, Charleston, South Carolina

Split 1 banana lengthwise and place the halves parallel on a round platter. Place 1 large scoop of vanilla ice cream between the banana halves. Cut 2 Krispy Kreme glazed doughnuts in half and place the pieces around the ice cream. Ladle 3 ounces of hot fudge over all, and garnish with raspberry whipped cream (raspberry puree folded into whipped cream).

Candied Banana Split

Emmanuel, Studio City, California

Split 1 banana lengthwise, and caramelize the halves in a pan over medium heat (see sidebar on page 58). Place the caramelized banana halves parallel on a round dish and put 1 scoop each of vanilla bean and chocolate–Mandarin orange ice cream between them. Ladle 2 ounces of caramel syrup over the vanilla bean and 2 ounces of chocolate syrup over the chocolate–Mandarin orange ice cream. Garnish with whipped cream, and sprinkle with pieces of walnut praline.

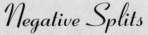

Negative Splits

If you watch a long-distance footrace, you'll see runners gobbling bananas before, during, and after the event. The banana provides portable, easy-to-eat, long-lasting energy, and it's not uncommon for a competitor in the Ironman Triathlon to consume as many as 20 bananas during the race.

His Banana Museum isn't simply the aggregation of three decades' worth of banana collecting. It's also a purposefully cultivated business and marketing tool. The storefront space in downtown Altadena is filled with a mélange of commercial products, folk art, and other cultural oddities devoted to the cheerful yellow fruit. It's an all-out banana assault. Spread out, posted, and piled to the rafters are such objects as banana telephones, books about bananas, banana-shaped candy, banana bucket bicycle seats, banana wristwatches, banana neckties, plush bananas, a blown-glass banana, and banana boxer shorts. One of the most utilitarian items is the banana-shaped golf putter. It comes with yellow golf balls.

There are bananas made of brass, glass, lead, wood, plastic, ceramic, cement, and soap. There are banana pipes, banana trees, pins, charms, belts, magnets, rings, cups, glasses, banana slicers, clocks, musical bananas, a "boudoir banana" from Italy, and an odd, gold-sequined "Michael Jackson Banana." Bannister can even show you what the world looks like through his yellow-tinted eyeglasses.

Those who worry about the vitality of Banana Split culture should consider some of Bannister's even more esoteric

Eat One for the Gipper

Melvin Stewart was the greatest 200-meter butterfly swimmer of his era, a gold medalist at the 1992 Olympics in Barcelona, Spain. Stewart's swimming career began in 1974. Under the direction of coach Frankie Bell at the Johnston Memorial YMCA pool in Charlotte, North Carolina, Stewart won national YMCA titles. Bell taught him stroke technique and motivated the already inspired youngster with a Banana Split every time he won. By the age of 10, he was ranked among the nation's top 10 in his age group in 16 events.

Big Bad Banana Split

The Charley Horse, West Bridgewater, Massachusetts

*P*lace 2 scoops of vanilla ice cream in a frosted 25-ounce glass mug, and ladle on 2 ounces of crushed strawberries. Add 2 scoops of chocolate ice cream, and ladle on 2 ounces of hot fudge. Split 1 banana lengthwise, then cut the split halves again widthwise. Arrange the banana quarters vertically around the ice cream, against the edge of the mug. Garnish with whipped cream in the center of the bananas, and place a whole cherry at the top.

Upside-Down Banana Split

Glen Dairy Bar, Watkins Glen, New York

*P*lace 1 scoop each of vanilla, chocolate, and strawberry ice cream in a Banana Split dish. Ladle 2 ounces of crushed pineapple over the vanilla, 2 ounces of chocolate syrup over the chocolate, and 2 ounces of crushed strawberries over the strawberry ice cream. Split 1 banana lengthwise and place the halves parallel on top of the ice cream. Garnish with whipped cream and chopped mixed nuts, and place a whole cherry at the top.

2001 Space Odyssey

The Rocket, Albany, New York

*S*plit 1 banana lengthwise and place the halves parallel on a round dish. Place 1 scoop each of vanilla and chocolate ice cream between the banana halves. Ladle 3 ounces of hot fudge over all. Garnish with whipped cream, sprinkle with chopped mixed nuts, and place a whole cherry at the top.

B.Y.O.B.

Bring your own banana to Bruster's Old Fashioned Ice Cream Shop on any Tuesday, and your Banana Split is half-price. The parlor in Pittsburgh, Pennsylvania, is owned by Don Oshop, whose bicycling exploits incloude a 20,000-mile, around-the-world tour. In 2002, Oshop set the world record on a stationary bicycle in the window of Bruster's, pedaling nonstop for 61 hours.

" **I am going back to my hotel, where I have a Banana Split waiting for me.** "

— **Marion Jones, after winning the 100-meter dash at the 2001 Goodwill Games**

" **The gray plodders running this thing make more money than a Banana Split salesman at an orangutan convention.** "

— **Andrew Bell of Globe Finance, recommending Enbridge stock at $38.95**

Banana Princess

When she was a child, her parents called her Anna Banana. But it was not until a 1980 trip to Hawaii, where she purchased her first banana artifact, that she recognized the seriousness of her passion. Years later, Ann Lovell presides over her own shameless treasure trove of banana memorabilia—whimsical, serious, and peculiar to the culture. Nearly 4,000 tropical fruit–related items are displayed throughout her home in Auburn, Washington, which was visited by director Kevin Smith for his "Roadside Attractions" segment on *The Tonight Show*. "He seemed particularly interested in the X-rated bananas," says Lovell. So what's her advice for others with a collecting urge? "Pick something you will like having around, not just something you think will be an investment. If you choose bananas, be prepared to hear the usual clichés, like 'going bananas' and 'they have a-peel.'"

Big Bang Banana Split

Mars 2112, New York, New York

*P*lace 1 scoop each of vanilla, chocolate, and strawberry ice cream in a homemade cookie shell (remove large baked cookie from oven and mold into shell while still hot by placing over a rolling pin). Split 1 banana lengthwise, then cut the split halves again widthwise. Rest the banana quarters along each side of the cookie shell. Ladle 2 ounces of raspberry puree over the vanilla, 2 ounces of chocolate syrup over the chocolate, and 2 ounces of crème anglaise over the strawberry ice cream. Garnish with whipped cream and sliced fresh strawberries.

Spumoni Banana Split

Gelato d'Italia, Denver, Colorado

*S*plit 1 banana lengthwise and place the halves parallel on a Banana Split dish. Place 1 scoop each of chocolate, strawberry, and pistachio gelato between the banana halves. Ladle 2 ounces of chocolate syrup and 2 ounces of mixed-berry puree between the scoops of gelato. Garnish with whipped cream, and place a whole cherry at the top.

Banana Split

Madison Bar & Grill, Hoboken, New Jersey

*S*plit 1 banana lengthwise, and caramelize the halves in a pan over medium heat (see sidebar on page 58). Place the caramelized banana halves parallel on a Banana Split dish and put 1 scoop each of vanilla, chocolate, and strawberry gelato between them. Ladle 3 ounces of chocolate syrup over all. Garnish with whipped cream, and sprinkle with chopped walnuts. Place slices of 1 large, fresh strawberry at the top, and dust them with powdered sugar.

items, including a fake-food Banana Split, scented Banana Split candles, sunless Banana Split tanning cream, bath salts, cologne, Banana Split-shaped teapots and cookie jars, Banana Split salt and pepper shakers, and Banana Split Christmas tree ornaments. And, of course, there are hundreds of Banana Split dishes in all shapes and forms.

Nearly buried in the all-too-full bloom of clutter is a yellow boom box that plays banana-inspired songs from a cassette tape Bannister put together. The selection includes Bannister favorites "I Like Bananas (Because They Have No Bones)" by the Hoosier Hot Shots, and, from the 1954 film *Top Banana*, "If You Want to Be Top Banana You Have to Start at the Bottom of the Bunch." Other selections include Louis Prima's renditions of "Banana Split for My Baby"

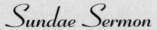

Sundae Sermon

In an episode of *The Simpsons*, Lisa Simpson visits an ice cream stall at the church fair. Above the stall is a banner declaring, "A Sundae Service You Can Swallow," and the ice cream flavors on sale have religious names, including Buddhist Banana Split and Virgin Mary Knickerbocker Glory. "You can even have a Unitarian ice cream," says the Reverend Lovejoy. "Oh, I'll have one of those," says Lisa. When presented with just the bowl, she exclaims, "But there's nothing in it!" "Exactly," says the Reverend Lovejoy.

Hot Fudge Bonanza Split

Swensen's, San Francisco, California

Split 1 banana lengthwise and place the halves parallel on a Banana Split dish. Place 2 scoops of vanilla ice cream between the banana halves. Ladle 2 ounces of hot fudge over one scoop and 2 ounces of hot butterscotch over the other. Garnish with whipped cream, sprinkle with toasted almonds, and place a whole cherry at the top.

Split Decision

Death by Chocolate, Vancouver, British Columbia

Split 1 banana lengthwise, and caramelize the halves in a pan over medium heat (see sidebar on page 58). Roll the caramelized banana halves in crumbled Oreo cookies. Place the banana halves parallel at the bottom of a chocolate shell (available at gourmet food stores) and put 2 scoops of vanilla ice cream between them. Ladle 2 ounces of crushed pineapple over one scoop and 2 ounces of chocolate syrup over the other. Garnish with chocolate mousse or whipped cream with shaved chocolate, stick 3 pirouette cookies into the top, and dust with powdered sugar.

Cosmic Banana Split

Sophie's Cosmic Café, Vancouver, British Columbia

Split 1 banana lengthwise and place the halves parallel on a Banana Split dish. Place 2 scoops of vanilla ice cream between the banana halves. Place slices of 6 fresh strawberries over the ice cream, and ladle 3 ounces of chocolate syrup over all. Garnish with whipped cream, sprinkle with toasted almonds, and place slices of fresh kiwi at the top.

Just Say No

2C-B is a psychoactive substance that produces euphoria and increased auditory, visual, olfactory, and tactile sensations. It is clandestinely produced as a powder, then pressed into pills or inserted into capsules for oral ingestion, although it also can be snorted. When users consume 2C-B with other illicit drugs including LSD, the combination is referred to as a Banana Split.

Split Screen

"One banana, two banana, three banana, four . . . ." The Saturday-morning kids' show called *The Banana Splits Adventure Hour* was a landmark in 1960s TV, combining live action, costumed hijinks, classic animation, rock music, and 20 minutes of cereal commercials.

> **Watching *Casino Royale* for me is like devouring a Banana Split. I should know better, but after that first gooey, sweet bite, I'm hooked for the entire dessert.**
>
> — **Ed Peters, Film Critic**

> **It's like a Banana Split topped with anchovies.**
>
> — **Bill Miller, editor of the *Blue Chip Radio Report*, on the Country Music Association's plan to move the annual awards show out of Nashville**

Another Fine Mess

In *Men O' War*, Stan Laurel and Oliver Hardy play sailors trying to impress two girls they meet in a soda shop. They are arguing about how they have enough money for only 3 sodas and Stan must refuse one, but he keeps saying he wants a soda too, then finally concedes, "I don't want any." One of the girls says, "Oh, General—don't be a piker!" Stan replies, "All right, I'll have a Banana Split!"

Dr. Bob's Dainty Banana Split

Brentwood Restaurant and Lounge, Brentwood, California

Split 1 baby banana and place the halves parallel at the bottom of a Burgundy wine glass. Place 1 scoop of Tahitian vanilla ice cream between the banana halves. Ladle 2 ounces of chocolate syrup over the ice cream. Garnish with whipped cream, sprinkle with toasted almonds, and place a pignoli (pine nut) cookie at the top.

Bistro Banana Split

Brick Oven Bistro, Boise, Idaho

Split 1 banana lengthwise and place the halves parallel on a Banana Split dish. Place 2 scoops of French vanilla ice cream between the banana halves. Ladle 2 ounces of bourbon-walnut sauce (see sidebar) over one scoop and 2 ounces of hot fudge over the other. Garnish with whipped cream, sprinkle with chopped mixed nuts, and place a whole cherry at the top.

Bourbon-Walnut Sauce

2 tablespoons butter
1 cup toasted walnuts, chopped
2/3 cup brown sugar
6 tablespoons bourbon
3/4 cup heavy cream
3 tablespoons milk
1 tablespoon cornstarch

Melt the butter in a saucepan over medium heat. Add the walnuts, stirring constantly. Add the brown sugar and cook until melted. Remove pan from heat and add the bourbon one tablespoon at a time. Add the cream, return pan to heat, and bring to a slow boil. Combine milk and cornstarch. Add the milk mixture to the sauce, stirring constantly until thickened.

Banana Split

Maraskino, Rancho Mirage, California

Split 1 banana lengthwise and place the halves in a chocolate tortilla bowl (a chocolate-flavored tortilla molded into the shape of a bowl). Place 1 scoop each of vanilla, chocolate, and strawberry ice cream between the banana halves, and ladle 3 ounces of caramel syrup over all. Garnish with whipped cream and sprinkle with Brazil nuts. Place the tortilla bowl on a 12-inch round platter and surround the entire dessert with cherry-flavored cotton candy.

> **A Beethoven symphony is not a kind of musical Banana Split, a matter of purely sensuous enjoyment.**
>
> — From *Emotion and Meaning in Music* by Leonard B. Meyer

and "Please No Squeeza Da Banana," "Loving You Has Made Me Bananas" by Guy Marks, Harry Chapin's "Thirty Thousand Pounds of Bananas," Madonna's "I'm Going Bananas," Siouxsie and the Banshees' "Christine, the Banana Split Lady," and "The Banana Split Polka."

"There is something about the banana that makes us laugh and keeps our spirits up," insists Bannister, as he taps his feet to the music. "The mere look of a banana and the sound of the word are funny."

There is a sublime absurdity in the idea of a museum devoted to a single fruit, but there is a lot of winning sentimentality to be found in Bannister's world. We ought to be grateful for his industriousness, his thoroughness, and his implicit desire to make a positive

The Truth Is Out There

UFO-debunker Robert Sheaffer has examined photographic evidence in some of the highest-profile UFO cases, and he has shown how easy it is to make fake pictures of unidentified flying objects. He has uncovered creations made with two aluminum plates; a cottage cheese container and a pie plate; and a Banana Split dish with modeling clay.

Mellow Yellow

Back in the 1960s an urban legend circulated claiming that if you baked a banana peel in an oven and scraped the inside of it, you could roll it into a joint and smoke it for a pot-like high.

Stage Left Banana Split

Stage Left Restaurant, New Brunswick, New Jersey

Slice 1 banana into disks and "shingle" them around the outside of a round platter. Sprinkle the banana disks with sugar and heat them with a small butane blowtorch or under a broiler until the sugar melts and caramelizes (see sidebar on page 58). Place a thin ginger cookie in the center, top it with 1 large scoop of softened Tahitian vanilla ice cream, and place a second cookie on top to form a sandwich. Ladle melted Valrhona chocolate around the edge of the platter, garnish the cookie sandwich with whipped cream, and place a whole bourbon-marinated cherry at the top.

ABC Banana Split

ABC Café, Ithaca, New York

Split 1 banana lengthwise and place the halves parallel on a Banana Split dish. Place 1 scoop each of vanilla and chocolate ice cream between the banana halves. Ladle 2 ounces of maple syrup over the vanilla and 2 ounces of chocolate syrup over the chocolate ice cream. Garnish with whipped cream, and sprinkle with granola.

Banana Sorbet Split

Gordon's House of Fine Eats, San Francisco, California

Split 1 banana lengthwise, sprinkle the halves with brown sugar, and heat them with a small butane blowtorch or under a broiler until the sugar melts and caramelizes (see sidebar on page 58). Place the banana halves in a large white bowl and add 1 scoop each of coconut, mango, and guava sorbet. Ladle 4 ounces of a compote of mango, pineapple, tangerine, and lime slices, all marinated overnight with sugar, over all. Sprinkle with toasted coconut.

Slippery Slope

The banana has been a prop on stage and screen for generations, propelling comedians into head-over-heels antics and guaranteeing guffaws.

In Abbott and Costello's *Hit the Ice,* Lou mistakenly finds a banana in his pocket instead of a gun. During the football-game climax in the Marx Brothers' *Horse Feathers,* Harpo trips up the opposing team by tossing banana peels under their feet. At the finale of *It's a Mad Mad Mad Mad World,* Ethel Merman ingloriously slips on a banana peel, while in Woody Allen's futuristic *Sleeper,* our hero escapes his pursuers by leaving a trail of peels from a 10-foot banana. And an orangutan named Suzanne shares a Banana Split with the two main characters in Kevin Smith's *Jay and Silent Bob Strike Back.*

Human Banana Split

On the Nickelodeon cable channel's game show "Double Dare 2000," Arthur Witt's children threw bananas at him while his wife poured whipped cream and chocolate syrup over his head. "It's down my shorts and everything," said Witt.

> **❝ The Doors without [Jim] Morrison is a Banana Split with no banana. ❞**
>
> **— Writer Zac Shaw, on the reconstituted band's 2003 tour**

Handy Advice

Model Dawn Gallagher, author of *Naturally Beautiful: Earth's Secrets and Recipes for Skin, Body, and Spirit,* cares for chapped or cracking hands with what she calls the Banana Split Hand Treatment: Mix up half of a ripe banana, $\frac{1}{2}$ teaspoon honey, and a few drops of vitamin E, rub the mixture over your hands, put on a pair of cotton gloves, and wear overnight.

Black Russian Banana Split

Grillfish, Boston, Massachusetts

*P*lace 3 scoops of vanilla ice cream in a large brandy snifter. Split 1 banana lengthwise, then cut the split halves again widthwise. Arrange the banana quarters vertically around the edge of the glass. Ladle 3 ounces of Kahlua-spiked hot fudge over the ice cream. Garnish with whipped cream, sprinkle with pecans, and place a whole cherry at the top.

Banana Split

Shallots, Chicago, Illinois

*P*lace an individual portion of banana streusel coffee cake on a Banana Split dish. Slice half a banana into disks, and caramelize the pieces in a pan over medium heat (see sidebar on page 58). Arrange the caramelized banana disks over the cake. Center 1 scoop each of banana, strawberry, and chocolate-brownie sorbet over the bananas. Top with toasted marshmallows and a pitted, chocolate-covered fresh cherry.

Banana Blitz

Fair Oaks Pharmacy and Soda Fountain, South Pasadena, California

*P*lace 2 scoops of vanilla ice cream on a Banana Split dish. Split 1 banana lengthwise and press the halves against each side of the ice cream. Dice a 3-inch-square brownie into small pieces and sprinkle them over the ice cream. Ladle on 2 ounces of hot fudge, garnish with whipped cream, and place a whole cherry at the top.

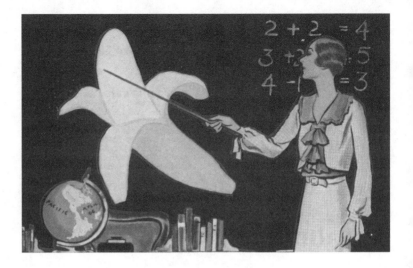

difference in people's lives. Noel Coward once said that work is "more fun than fun." If nothing else, this banana zealot to end all banana zealots has put some fun back into the profession of selling.

"I've done more to promote the banana than any one individual in the whole world," says the never modest Bannister. "I prove you can have your cliché and eat it, too."

Flower Power

The American Horticultural Society has identified a thoroughbred daylily, with a pointed, elongated bud that opens to show six yellow-cream petals. It is called the Savannah Banana Split.

Toasted Pound Cake Banana Split Sundae

Sarabeth's, New York, New York

Place 1 slice of purchased pound cake, lightly grilled or toasted, in a dessert bowl. Split 1 banana lengthwise and place the halves parallel on top of the cake. Place 1 scoop of vanilla ice cream between the banana halves. Strain 4 ounces of blueberry preserves, and pour them over the ice cream. Garnish with whipped cream, and sprinkle with shaved chocolate, toasted coconut, and chopped mixed nuts.

Organic Banana Split

Sprout Café, Roswell, Georgia

Split 1 organically grown banana lengthwise and place the halves parallel on a Banana Split dish. Place 2 scoops of vanilla "nice cream" (a nondairy frozen dessert) between the banana halves. Ladle 2 ounces of carob syrup over all, sprinkle with chopped mixed nuts, and place slices of organically grown strawberries at the top.

St. Lucia Snooze

Calypso Raw Bar & Restaurant, Pompano Beach, Florida

Split 1 banana lengthwise and place the halves parallel on a Banana Split dish. Place 1 scoop each of vanilla and chocolate ice cream between the banana halves. Ladle 3 ounces of warm buttered-rum sauce over all (to make sauce, stir $1\frac{1}{2}$ ounces of hot water, $1\frac{1}{2}$ ounces of rum, and 1 tablespoon of butter until the butter has melted). Garnish with whipped cream, and sprinkle with toasted almonds.

Hi Ho, Steverino!

As TV's first host of *The Tonight Show*, Steve Allen kept America up past its bedtime with antics like turning himself into a 6-foot-3 Banana Split. He added to his legend with a staggering output of 5,200 musical compositions, including "Banana Split," recorded in 1957 by the McGuire Sisters.

Key Words

Banana Boat. Refers to an elongated or "boat-shaped" dish, designed and manufactured for the service of Banana Splits. First made by the Westmoreland Glass Company in 1904, and produced continuously through 1984. By the 1920s, Anchor Hocking had produced a "footed" version in glass, and in 1946, Tablecraft introduced a stainless-steel model.

❝ This is a Banana Split . . . and it's quite possibly one of the greatest things in the universe. **❞**

— Deanna Troi, *Star Trek: The Next Generation*

❝ Why don't we just skip the wine and have a Banana Split? **❞**

— Lucy, at the Stop the Ghostwood Development wine-tasting soiree, *Twin Peaks* episode 26

Don't Mess with Texas

Blue Bell, the little creamery in Brenham, Texas, that began making butter back in 1907 and switched to ice cream four years later, is now the biggest brand in the state and the third-largest ice cream maker in America, behind national brands Breyer's and Dreyer's. According to Steve James, Blue Bell's vice president, Banana Split is the most labor-intensive flavor the company makes. It requires vanilla ice cream to be mixed with maraschino cherries, pineapple chunks, strawberry topping, chocolate syrup, nuts, and sliced bananas. Eight workers sit along a small conveyor belt, peeling fresh bananas right out of a Chiquita box and slicing them into quarter-inch pieces. "We've tested it so that when you dip out a scoop of Banana Split," explains James, "each serving will have at least one slice of banana in it."

Baby Banana Sundae

Pacific East, Amagansett, New York

Split 2 baby bananas lengthwise and place the halves on a round platter so that they form an X. At the center of the X place 1 scoop of caramel ice cream. Ladle 2 ounces of chocolate syrup over the ice cream. Garnish with whipped cream, and sprinkle with macadamia nuts.

Sunshine Split

Leiby's Ice Cream House, Tamaqua, Pennsylvania

Split 1 banana lengthwise and place the halves parallel on a Banana Split dish. Place 1 scoop each of vanilla ice cream and orange sherbet between the banana halves. Ladle 2 ounces of crushed pineapple over the vanilla ice cream and 2 ounces of marshmallow creme over the orange sherbet. Garnish with whipped cream, and place a whole cherry at the top.

To Blue or Not to Blue Banana Split

Lithia Fountain & Grill, Ashland, Oregon

Split 1 banana lengthwise and place the halves parallel on a Banana Split dish. Place 3 scoops of vanilla ice cream between the banana halves. Pour 1 cup of fresh blueberries over the ice cream, and garnish with whipped cream.

Chapter 7

New World Order

> **You see things; and you say, "Why?" But I dream things that never were; and I say, "Why not?"**
>
> — **George Bernard Shaw**

From David Strickler's own day to the present, his Banana Split has been subjected to innumerable interpretations. Not everyone, it seems, is enslaved to a single formula. Some believe the original is a style better left to Grandma—or to Great-Great-Grandma. Today, when cuisine has become something of a competitive sport, the best Splits are likely to take the form of novel, innovative creations by a new breed of culinary originators. Nowhere is the urge to reinvent greater than in the kitchens of our fashionable restaurants.

Ah, Norman! There aren't many men in South Florida, or women for that matter, with whom everyone is on a first-name basis, but Chef Norman Van Aken is one of them. His restaurant, Norman's, in Coral Gables, is renowned for embracing the historical influences that South and Central America and the Caribbean have had on American cooking.

Deconstructing the Split

"I am striving to change the way we think about dessert and bring attention to what I think is a very artistic medium," says Elizabeth Faulkner, proprietor of a San Francisco mecca of decadence called Citizen Cake and one of the most celebrated pastry chefs in the United States. The self-described "deconstructivist" draws on her filmmaking background when composing food or designing a recipe, and her unique vision borrows from the vertical schematic of the parfait to create an artful Banana Split. From a base of sliced bananas, she builds a multitude of flavors, textures, and colors, with layers of chocolate sorbet, vanilla ice cream, banana bread, homemade marshmallow, fudge sauce, caramel, strawberry *pâté de fruit*, cocoa nibs, almonds, and maraschino foam. This tedious effort, she says, is liberating. Explains Ms. Faulkner, "I just wanted to present it in a way that represents how we eat today."

A professional contemporary, Emeril Lagasse, calls Van Aken "one of America's greatest and most innovative chefs, whose fusion of flavors and cultures explodes in your palate.

But you can't merely label Norman Van Aken a "celebrity chef." Writer Daniel Boorstin contends that "celebrities are people who make the news, but heroes are people who make history." For his lifelong contributions to the culture of his region, Van Aken was selected by the *St. Petersburg Times* as "one of the 25 people who mattered the most in Florida's history." You've got to think of him as a local hero.

He has an uncomplicated but brilliant mind, which, fortunately, has not been "improved" by cooking school. His food is a tropical melting pot, and he eloquently voices his culinary philosophy: "If a map of the world were a tablecloth, and I could choose a place at that table, I would sit at the southern tip of Florida, at the nexus of

Split Infinitive

Pauline Kael, the prolific and enduring film critic for the *New Yorker*, was not the magazine's typical writer. Her descriptions were sometimes a bit too pedestrian for the literati. Once, when she wanted to describe the sets of a movie as reminiscent of a Banana Split, her editor insisted on changing the comparison to a pousse-café (an after-dinner drink made by layering several liqueurs).

Havana Banana Split

Norman's, Coral Gables, Florida
Chef Norman Van Aken

For the chile jelly:

2 ancho chiles, stems and seeds discarded

2 chipotle chiles, stems and seeds discarded

6 tablespoons red currant jelly

6 tablespoons honey

2 tablespoons Spanish sherry wine vinegar

For the bananas:

7 ripe bananas, peeled

2½ tablespoons butter

1 tablespoon dark brown sugar

3 tablespoons Myers's dark rum
(or any dark rum)

6 scoops premium-quality store-bought or homemade vanilla ice cream

Your favorite chocolate syrup, to taste, warmed

❶ To make the chile jelly, toast the chile skins in a dry skillet until you can smell their earthy heat.

❷ Put the toasted chile skins in a saucepan with 1 quart of water and simmer on medium heat until the water is almost completely evaporated. Add the currant jelly, honey, and vinegar. Bring to a boil. Remove from the heat and process thoroughly in a food processor. Remove to a clean bowl and cool.

❸ To prepare the bananas, cut them into ¼-inch-thick slices. Heat a skillet to moderately hot. Place the bananas in the skillet with the butter and brown sugar. When the butter is melted, add 2 tablespoons of the prepared chile jelly. Toss the bananas to coat them. Remove the bananas, then add the rum to the pan and carefully deglaze.

❹ Place a scoop of ice cream in the center of each of 6 shallow bowls. Arrange the bananas around the ice cream. Drizzle with warm chocolate syrup.

You Must Remember This

During Hollywood's heyday, the Brown Derby was *the* gathering place for the movie colony's biggest and brightest stars. Although the original joint closed in 1985 after 57 years of operation, a replica of the Brown Derby has been installed at the MGM Grand Casino in Las Vegas. The Brown Derby's signature Banana Split is served in a molded chocolate derby hat, the top of which lifts off to reveal three scoops of ice cream, bananas, sauces, and berries.

" The elegant clotheshorse wears the world's ugliest dress—it looks like a giant Banana Split, with oversized marshmallows for triceps. "

**— Film critic Richard Corliss, describing
Barbara Stanwyck in *Stella Dallas***

" I look forward to the month of July when summer days will swelter. I envision sitting in the shade of a tree eating a cold Banana Split, dripping with whipped cream and chopped nuts, and watching carefully the bird in the branches overhead, making sure the only thing 'dripping' is ice cream. "

— Scott O. Graham, writer

Balanced Diet

The ancient philosophy of balance and harmony inspired a chain of Chinese restaurants to create an Asian Banana Split. There are 84 P. F. Chang's China Bistros, all serving Banana Spring Rolls for dessert—a contrast of hot and cold, yin and yang, on one plate. A ripe banana is split widthwise into six 2-inch sections, each of which is dusted with five different Chinese spices and sugar, wrapped in spring roll wrappers, then deep-fried. The banana rolls are placed around a large scoop of coconut-pineapple ice cream, then drizzled with caramel and vanilla syrups. It leaves yin where there was once yang, and yang where there was once yin.

Banana Lumpia Split

Renaissance Ilikai Hotel, Waikiki, Hawaii

Chef Chip Hawkins

4 ounces semisweet chocolate, chopped fine

1 teaspoon peeled fresh ginger, minced fine

5 ounces adzuki beans, mashed

3 bananas, peeled

6 lumpia (Filipino egg roll) wrappers

$\frac{1}{4}$ cup all-purpose flour

2 eggs, beaten

6 scoops macadamia nut ice cream

6 tablespoons chocolate syrup

$\frac{3}{4}$ cup whipped cream

6 mint leaves

❶ Melt the chocolate with the minced ginger. Add the melted chocolate mixture to the mashed adzuki beans and mix well. If not to be used immediately, refrigerate until needed.

❷ Split the bananas lengthwise. Place 1 banana half on each lumpia wrapper and trim the ends of the bananas to fit, if necessary. Spread 2 to 3 tablespoons of the chocolate mixture over each banana half.

❸ Mix the flour and eggs together to make a paste, and spread a thin layer around the edge of each lumpia wrapper. Wrap the lumpia wrappers around the banana halves and seal the edges well.

❹ Deep-fry the banana lumpia at 375° F until crispy.

❺ Place 1 scoop of ice cream in the center of a banana boat. Cut each banana lumpia in half across the center and arrange one half on each side of the ice cream in each dish.

❻ Drizzle each dessert with chocolate syrup and top with 2 tablespoons of the whipped cream. Garnish with a mint leaf.

❝ That's too bad, girlies. I'm awfully sorry my boys were a little rough. What say we all go down to the corner for a double Banana Split and a fistful of chocolate eclairs? **❞**

— George Halas, Chicago Bears owner–coach, after his team crushed the Washington Redskins, 31–7 in 1938

❝ Chefs are discovering their inner mall-rats and serving up the king of all-American desserts, the Banana split. **❞**

— Katy McLaughlin, *The Wall Street Journal*

North America and the Caribbean. My plate would touch Cuba, the Florida Keys, the Yucatan, the West Indies, the Bahamas, and South America. And, if time could tell, I would listen to the tales of voyagers, discoverers, traders, and mystics who, in searching for 'the Indies,' the great Khan and the riches of China, discovered something much more valuable and enduring—a new world of culinary treasures."

An agile, versatile technician, Van Aken eschews high drama, and instead depends on instincts he developed as a boy, cooking and canning at his hard-working mother's side. During his early tadpolehood in Diamond Lake, Illinois, he

Cinnamon-Grilled Bananas with Mexican Chocolate

Frontera Grill/Topolobampo, Chicago, Illinois
Chef Rick Bayless

4 firm but ripe bananas, unpeeled
1 tablespoon sugar
½ teaspoon ground cinnamon (preferably Mexican cinnamon, or *canela*)
8 small scoops dulce de leche ice cream
½ cup coarsely chopped Mexican chocolate

❶ Slice the bananas in half lengthwise, then cut the split halves again widthwise. Set the banana quarters aside.

❷ Combine the sugar and cinnamon, and sprinkle on the cut sides of the bananas. Let bananas sit for 5 minutes.

❸ Place bananas, cut side down, on a clean cooking grate. Cook for 2 minutes or until grill marks appear.

❹ Using a pair of long-handled tongs, turn the bananas over and let cook 5 more minutes or until the peel pulls away from the banana. Carefully remove the peels.

❺ Arrange 4 banana quarters on each serving plate. Top each serving with 2 scoops of ice cream. Sprinkle each with 1 tablespoon of the chopped chocolate.

❝❝ Three baths and a Banana Split later I'm feeling all right. ❞❞

— Daniella Westbrook, *I'm a Celebrity . . . Get Me Out of Here* contestant, on leaving the Australian rain forest

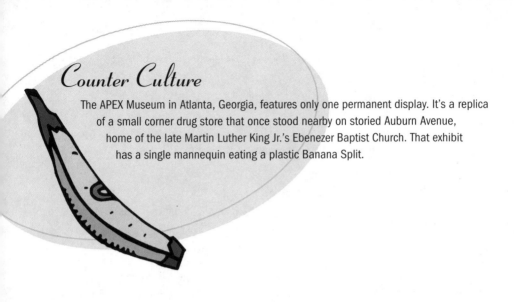

Counter Culture

The APEX Museum in Atlanta, Georgia, features only one permanent display. It's a replica of a small corner drug store that once stood nearby on storied Auburn Avenue, home of the late Martin Luther King Jr.'s Ebenezer Baptist Church. That exhibit has a single mannequin eating a plastic Banana Split.

often accompanied his grandmother as she conducted guided tours of Hawthorne Melody Farms, his hometown dairy. The tours always ended with a sample of the dairy's ice cream, and it was the beginning of young Norman's love affair with dessert.

After dropping out of college, he worked in several restaurants before he was taken under the wing of legendary Chicago restaurateur Gordon Sinclair, one of the earliest proponents of New American cuisine. Well known for his wit and sophistication, Sinclair was a consummate professional, who, according to Van Aken, "taught me a profound respect for ingredients and gave me the freedom to follow my passion."

As his palate expanded, so did his horizons. Van Aken found a path to South Florida, where he was seduced by the cross-cultural culinary landscape. He left his mark in several kitchens around Miami before opening Norman's in 1995. It was there, while exploring and blending the ethnic flavors from a broad palette of influences, that Van Aken coined the term *fusion cooking*, and unlocked the secrets of a brave new culinary world.

> **Every culture has its own flavor profiles; ours is represented by the big, brash Banana Split.**
>
> — **Rick Bayless,**
> **author and restaurateur**

"Baanahna" Royale

Britain's Queen Elizabeth and her husband Prince Philip knew each other as children. But their official courtship got its start in the Captain's House in Dartmouth in 1939, when young princess Elizabeth, in the words of the royal governess, "fell in love with Philip over shrimps and Banana Splits."

Caramelized Pistachio and Brown Sugar Banana Split

Lonesome Dove Western Bistro, Fort Worth, Texas

Chef Tim Love

For the pancake batter:

2½ cups flour

½ cup sugar

½ teaspoon kosher salt

5 whole eggs

3 egg yolks

2 cups milk

1 tablespoon vanilla extract

1 tablespoon liqueur of your choice

2 tablespoons butter

For the chocolate ganache:

1 pint heavy cream

12 ounces semisweet chocolate chips

For the bananas and sauce:

4 bananas, peeled and split lengthwise

½ cup brown sugar

½ cup pistachios, ground

2 ounces Tuaca

To cook the pancakes:

1 ounce Kahlúa

3 tablespoons unsalted butter

8 ounces vanilla bean ice cream

❶ To make the pancake batter, sift the flour, sugar, and salt together, then set aside.

❷ Using a wooden spoon, beat the whole eggs, one at a time. Add the egg yolks one at a time, beating well after each addition.

❸ Add the milk, vanilla, and liqueur to the eggs.

❹ Add the flour mixture and beat well.

❺ Melt 2 tablespoons butter in a sauté pan and cook over low heat until butter turns light brown, then blend it into the batter.

❻ Refrigerate the batter for 2 hours before using.

❼ To make the chocolate ganache, heat the cream until it boils, then add the chocolate chips. Remove from heat and stir until mixture is smooth. Set aside.

❽ To prepare the bananas and sauce, preheat a sauté pan and add the bananas, brown sugar, pistachios, and Tuaca. Simmer over low heat for 5 minutes.

❾ To cook the pancakes, mix the Kahlúa evenly into 2 cups of the pancake batter (reserve the remaining batter for future use). In a nonstick pan or on a griddle, melt 3 tablespoons butter over medium heat. Pour approximately 3 tablespoons of batter into the pan for each of 4 pancakes (each pancake should be about 3 inches in diameter). When bubbles form on the surface of the batter, turn the pancakes and cook until both sides are golden brown.

❿ Using a cookie cutter, cut the pancakes into the shape of Texas, if desired.

⓫ Cross 2 banana halves on a plate and cover with sauce. Add 1 scoop of ice cream, and top with a pancake. Cover with chocolate ganache. Repeat with remaining ingredients.

Banana Beignet Split

Asia SF, San Francisco, California

Chef Matthew Metcalf

For the chocolate fudge sauce:
1 cup heavy cream
1 cup sugar
¼ cup unsweetened cocoa powder
½ teaspoon vanilla extract
4 ounces corn syrup
4 ounces unsweetened chocolate, chopped
4 ounces semisweet chocolate, chopped

For the butterscotch sauce:
1 pound brown sugar
6 ounces corn syrup
4 ounces butter
2 ounces water
2 ounces milk
4 ounces heavy cream
⅛ teaspoon salt
3 ounces butterscotch chips

For the macadamia nut brittle:
6 cups macadamia nuts
4 cups sugar
1 teaspoon salt
8 ounces butter

For the banana beignets:
6 bananas, peeled
3 ounces butter
¼ teaspoon salt
¾ cup sugar
¼ cup brandy
1 egg, beaten
16 lumpia (Filipino egg roll) wrappers
Canola oil, for frying

For the caramelized baby bananas:
8 baby bananas, peeled and sliced lengthwise
6 tablespoons sugar

8 scoops vanilla ice cream

Maraschino cherries

❶ To make the chocolate fudge sauce, in a heavy-bottomed saucepot over medium heat mix the cream, sugar, cocoa powder, vanilla, and 4 ounces corn syrup until the mixture is very hot but not boiling.

❷ Add the unsweetened and semisweet chocolate and whisk until the mixture is smooth. Set aside.

❸ To make the butterscotch sauce, combine the brown sugar, 6 ounces corn syrup, 4 ounces butter, and water in a heavy-bottomed saucepot and cook over medium heat until the temperature of the mixture reaches 240°F.

❹ Let the mixture cool slightly, until it is warm but not hot, and whisk in the remaining ingredients until the mixture is smooth. Set aside.

❺ To make the macadamia nut brittle, spread the nuts on a sheet pan and toast in the oven at 325°F until they are a light golden brown. Chop the nuts by hand or by pulsing briefly in a food processor.

❻ In a saucepot, heat the sugar, stirring until it liquefies and turns golden brown. Add the salt and 8 ounces butter. Add the chopped macadamia nuts and stir until coated. Using a heavy wooden rolling pin, spread the mixture on a sheet pan and let cool. When cool, break into small pieces by wrapping in a piece of cheesecloth and hammering with a kitchen mallet.

❼ To make the banana beignets, slice the bananas into $\frac{1}{3}$-inch-thick disks. Melt 3 ounces butter in a sauté pan over medium heat. Add the banana pieces and cook until they begin to soften.

❽ Add the salt, sugar, and brandy to the bananas. Remove the mixture from the heat and let cool.

❾ When the banana mixture is cool, place 4 tablespoons in the center of 1 lumpia wrapper and roll as you would a spring roll. Seal the edge of the wrapper with a little of the beaten egg. Repeat with the remaining lumpia wrappers.

❿ In a heavy-bottomed saucepot, heat canola oil to 360°F. Fry the banana beignets until they turn golden brown.

⓫ To make the caramelized baby bananas, place the sliced baby bananas on a metal sheet pan, cut side up. Sprinkle the sugar on the cut side of the bananas and caramelize with a small butane blowtorch or by placing under a broiler for a few minutes.

⓬ To assemble the Splits, cut the banana beignets in half diagonally. Place 1 scoop of ice cream in each of 8 bowls. Arrange 4 pieces of the banana beignets, cut side up, around each scoop of ice cream. Top with chocolate fudge and butterscotch sauces, 2 caramelized baby banana halves, crushed macadamia nut brittle, and maraschino cherries.

While shock jocks of the culinary world constantly strive for the next avant-garde combination, Eric and Bruce Bromberg's always mobbed Blue Ribbon restaurants prove that New Yorkers still yearn for traditional fried chicken, cheeseburgers, and Banana Splits.

According to Eric, "Every ingredient means something in a Banana Split." Perfect scoops of vanilla and chocolate ice cream are placed on either side of a scoop of strawberry and supported by split banana halves. Hot fudge is ladled between the chocolate and strawberry, hot butterscotch between the strawberry and vanilla. ("We skip the pineapple," says Eric. "It's too tart, too sweet.") Finishing touches include freshly whipped cream, chopped walnuts, and a cherry.

"Bless Blue Ribbon restaurants for respecting the perfection of the Banana Split," writes *New York Magazine*.

Some chefs merely cook. Others, like Van Aken, generate a special kind of enthusiasm for anything they prepare. Van Aken takes advantage of the foolproof model to create a beguiling Banana Split that is both a natural evolution of the classic dessert and a full realization of his unmistakable style. He calls it "a Cuban cousin to Bananas Foster," and it's easy to see why the Havana Banana Split is a hot ticket. The dessert is a subtle synopsis of how several influences can be seamlessly merged into one surefire recipe. It's a little bit pop, a little bit poetic.

"At the end of the day, few things are more gratifying to the eye and the imagination than a Banana Split," observes Van Aken. "Shape, form, and the way components play off each other take on new meaning in the overall sensory experience."

Peachy Keen Grilled Banana Split

St. Supery Vineyards and Winery, Rutherford, California
Chef Sunny Cristadoro-Groom

¼ cup sliced almonds
8 ounces fresh or frozen peaches
2 ounces St. Supery Moscato
1 tablespoon brown sugar
½ teaspoon cinnamon
1 tablespoon honey
1 tablespoon lemon juice
6 bananas
2 pints vanilla ice cream

❶ Toast the almond slices on a sheet pan in the oven at 350° F for about 7 minutes, or until golden. Set aside.

❷ In a food processor, combine the peaches, Moscato, brown sugar, and cinnamon. Puree until smooth. Set aside.

❸ Mix the honey and lemon juice in a small bowl.

❹ Cut the bananas in half lengthwise, leaving the skin on. Brush the cut side of each banana with the honey mixture and place, cut side down, on the grill.

❺ Cook until grill marks appear and the bananas soften slightly. Flip the bananas over and grill on the skin side for another minute or two. Remove from the grill.

❻ Peel the bananas and put two halves in each of 6 bowls. Add a scoop or two of ice cream and top with the peach sauce and toasted almonds.

" **Accountability is to leadership what a banana is to a Banana Split.** "

— **Michael Montgomery,**
Michigan Department of Corrections

Caribbean-Style Herb-Roasted Banana Split

SERVES 4

Globe Cafe by Moonlight, Salt Lake City, Utah

Chef Adam Kreisel

For the candied macadamia nuts:

1 cup raw whole unsalted macadamia nuts

1 cup granulated sugar

½ cup unsalted butter

For the brandied apricots:

½ cup (about 12 pieces) dried apricots

½ cup cooking brandy

For the rosemary whipped cream:

Leaves from 2 large sprigs fresh rosemary

2 cups heavy whipping cream

2 teaspoons powdered sugar

For the bananas:

4 whole baby red bananas (these should be ripe but still relatively firm; yellow bananas may be substituted, if necessary)

¼ cup unsalted butter, melted

8 to 10 4-inch sprigs fresh thyme

½ to ¾ cup light or dark brown sugar

vanilla extract

1 pint mocha ice cream

1 pint dulce de leche ice cream

Seeds of 1 whole pomegranate

1 bottle pomegranate molasses (available at Indian and some Middle Eastern markets)

1 bottle Whaler's dark rum (or any dark rum)

Several sprigs fresh mint (or peppermint), for garnish

❝ A Banana Split is probably the world's best food: cold ice cream, hot fudge, crunchy nuts, smooth cream. It's the world's perfect bite. It's got every texture. ❞

— Ming Tsai, celebrity chef

❶ To make the candied macadamia nuts, roast the macadamia nuts on a sheet pan in the oven at 325º F until they are a light golden brown. Remove the pan and increase the oven temperature to 375º F.

❷ In a small saucepot, heat the granulated sugar and $\frac{1}{2}$ cup butter together, stirring regularly until a golden caramel forms.

❸ Rough-chop the macadamia nuts by hand or by pulsing briefly in a food processor (you still want some big chunks) then drop them into the caramel. Stir briefly to mix, then remove the candied nuts to a sheet pan lined with waxed paper or parchment. Cool on the counter and reserve for use later.

❹ To prepare the brandied apricots, julienne the dried apricots. Place the cut fruit and the brandy in a small sauté pan or saucepot on low heat and allow the apricots to steep in the brandy until all of the liquid is gone. Remove from the heat, cool, and reserve.

❺ To make the rosemary whipped cream, finely mince the rosemary leaves. With a beater or by hand, whisk the whipping cream, minced rosemary, and powdered sugar together until the mixture forms soft peaks. Chill and reserve.

❻ To prepare the bananas, split them lengthwise, leaving the skin on, and lay them flat on a sheet pan. Brush the cut side of each banana with a small amount of the melted butter. Break the thyme sprigs into smaller pieces and place two or three small pieces on each banana half. Sprinkle each banana half with a liberal amount of brown sugar, using less or more depending on how much natural banana flavor you enjoy. Drizzle each banana half with a few drops of vanilla.

❼ Place the bananas in the oven and roast, uncovered, at 375° F for 7-9 minutes. (If you desire a sweeter, more caramelized flavor, roast the bananas for an extra minute or two.)

❽ Place 1 scoop each of mocha and dulce de leche ice cream in a bowl. Remove any remaining thyme sprigs from the bananas and crisscross two banana halves on top of the ice cream.

❾ Whisk the rosemary whipped cream for an additional 15 seconds and place a generous amount on top of the bananas.

❿ Place the candied macadamia nuts between two sheets of waxed paper and use a meat mallet or a small hammer to gently break them apart. Sprinkle some macadamia nuts, brandied apricots, and pomegranate seeds on the sundae.

⓫ Drizzle a small amount of pomegranate molasses and rum on top and garnish with sprigs of mint. Repeat with remaining ingredients.

He speaks eloquently about the luscious banana, and he uses a native Florida variety whenever they are available. "Once you add ice cream, sauces, and nuts to the fruit, the textural contrast is quite wonderful," says Van Aken. "Simple, humble, beautiful—this is why we love the Banana Split."

For now, the Havana Banana Split, with its unorthodox presentation, is a signature dish at Norman's, and, according to Van Aken, his guests have everything to do with that. "A signature dish is one that touches a nerve," he explains, "in the same way 'I Left My Heart in San Francisco' is Tony Bennett's signature song."

All of this proves that David Strickler's creation, so momentous in his own era, has no less resonance for his disciples today. The Banana Split tradition goes back a very long way, and contemporary, technically adept practitioners of culinary craftsmanship—even while setting trends—are keenly attuned to that tradition. Newfangled concoctions still fall back on the basic ingredients: bananas, ice cream, gooey sauces, nuts, whipped cream, sometimes even the cherry on top. Presentations, although imitative, are more exciting, ice cream flavors more exotic, sauces more eccentric. To some extent, it is a journey onward and upward.

But truth to tell, it's hard to improve on perfection. Norman Van Aken and his brethren in America's best kitchens cling tenaciously to their cherished memories of the primal recipe, so each new interpretation still seems familiar. Such is the ubiquity of the Banana Split.

Both Sides Now

"Why did the Banana Split cross the street?" Ask Christine Keff, chef/proprietor of Flying Fish and Fandango, two prominent Seattle eateries. Her dessert menu at Flying Fish offers a Banana Split Platter, with caramelized bananas; chocolate, strawberry, and banana ice cream; hot fudge and caramel sauce; and toasted house-made marshmallows. Served with pizzelle cookies and candied fresh cherries on a long rectangular platter, it's meant to be shared.

You need only walk across First Avenue for another side of the Banana Split, Ms. Keff's Latin-inspired version at Fandango. A ripe plantain is split, sprinkled with sugar, and grilled with the skin on. After the skin is removed, the plantain halves are crossed on a round dish, topped with vanilla ice cream, and bathed in a chocolate-chile sauce that dances in your mouth. "When it comes to dessert," says Ms. Keff, "you might say my customers have split loyalties."

Key Words

Plantain. A fruit that resembles the banana, except that it is more starchy than sweet, and typically not eaten raw; plantains are sometimes called "cooking bananas." Use plantains with peels that have darkened to brown or black as the base of a Banana Split.

The Split's Foster Child

A high-toned, southern-accented Banana Split called Bananas Foster is the house specialty at Brennan's in the French Quarter of New Orleans. In 1951, Chef Paul Blange arranged a perfect marriage of the tropical banana with rum, a tropical spirit, and turned it into a dish to honor Brennan's regular, Richard Foster. Brennan's now uses 35,000 pounds of bananas a year for the "haute Creole" dish that has gone on to become world famous.

Bananas Foster

SERVES 4

¼ cup (½ stick) butter

1 cup brown sugar

½ teaspoon cinnamon

¼ cup banana liqueur

4 bananas, each cut in half lengthwise, then halved again widthwise

¼ cup dark rum

4 large scoops vanilla ice cream (in serving bowls)

❶ Combine the butter, brown sugar, and cinnamon in a flambé pan or skillet. Place the pan over low heat either on an alcohol burner or on top of the stove, and cook, stirring, until the sugar dissolves.

❷ Stir in the banana liqueur, then place the bananas in the pan. When the banana sections soften and begin to brown, carefully add the rum. Continue to cook the sauce until the rum is hot, then ignite the rum with a long kitchen match or kitchen lighter.

❸ When the flames subside, lift the bananas out of the pan and place four pieces over each portion of ice cream.

❹ Generously spoon warm sauce over the top of the ice cream and serve immediately.

> **Now, it's quite simple to defend yourself against a man armed with a banana. First of all, you force him to drop the banana; then, second, you eat the banana, thus disarming him. You have now rendered him helpless.**
>
> — **John Cleese, in a *Monty Python's Flying Circus* skit**

The
FOOD VALUE
of the
BANANA

Chapter 8

The Original Comfort Food

> **What is patriotism but the love of food one ate as a child?**
>
> — Lin Yutang

Something about the banana lends itself to wistful nostalgia—something to do with childhood memories, the recollection of taste magnified through the prism of time. The banana first makes its way to American stomachs as gruel in the base of baby food, a bridge from mother's milk to solid food. The typical infant consumes 600 jars of baby food in his or her first 12 months, many containing bananas mashed into pulp. So throughout the rest of our lives, it's hard to resist getting all "warm and fuzzy" every time we eat a banana.

A banana is often eaten to calm digestive upset. Its nutritional virtues are highly touted, since it is rich in potassium, other essential trace elements, and tryptophan, an amino acid that the body converts into serotonin, which is believed to be a natural antidepressant. Since both bananas and ice cream have chemical and emotional triggers, it is probably no surprise that

Shaken, Not Stirred

An American cocktail craze is going strong, and bartenders have responded with a surge of "designer" martinis, including (why not?) the Banana Split Martini. While there are several formulas for the dessert-inspired drink, the River's Inn Restaurant in Gloucester Point, Virginia, has turned the tables to create a drink-inspired dessert. To make a Chocolate-Covered Banana Martini, mix one-quarter of a banana (sliced into pieces), 1 scoop of vanilla ice cream, $1\frac{1}{2}$ ounces espresso, 1 ounce amaretto, $\frac{1}{2}$ ounce vodka, and $\frac{1}{2}$ ounce dark crème de cacao in a blender. Swirl hot fudge around the inside of an oversize ice-cold martini glass, allow the fudge to harden, then pour in the banana mixture up to the rim. Garnish with a swirl of whipped cream and a drizzle of hot fudge. You'll find this "cocktail" on the dessert menu, not the drink list.

> **If I feel like a sweet, it's a Banana Split at Dairy Queen. No nuts, no whipped cream, no cherry. Just chocolate, pineapple, and strawberry sauce. Sometimes they freak out when I show up and put on more sauce, which is perfect for me.**

— **Celine Dion**

Split the Difference

PICK
A
BALLOON
JUMBO
BANANA
SPLIT
1¢ TO 39¢
TRY YOUR LUCK
WOOLWORTH'S

By the 1950s, the main street of virtually every town and city in the United States featured a Woolworth's 5 & 10, with a long, shiny lunch counter in the back of the store, and red-cushioned stools that spun around to raise or lower the seat. The store's special gimmick was a group of brightly colored balloons attached to long, thin sticks. When you placed your order for a Banana Split, the lady behind the counter in starched pink uniform would let you pop one of the balloons. Inside each balloon was a little piece of paper that determined your price, ranging from a penny to 39 cents.

Banana Split Nachos

Iron Horse, Portland, Oregon

Cut 2 flour tortillas into triangles, deep-fry at 375° F, then dust with sugar and cinnamon. Drain on paper towels and arrange on an oval platter. Split 1 banana lengthwise and place the halves parallel over the tortilla chips. Place 3 scoops of vanilla ice cream between the banana halves. Ladle 2 ounces of chocolate syrup over the first scoop, 2 ounces of caramel syrup over the second, and 2 ounces of crushed pineapple over the third. Garnish with whipped cream, and sprinkle with shaved dark chocolate.

Banana Split Dumplings

F. Scott's, Nashville, Tennessee

Split 1 banana lengthwise, then cut the split halves again widthwise. Combine the banana quarters with sliced mango, sliced papaya, sliced pineapple, cream cheese, and mascarpone cheese. Separate the mixture into 2 portions, and roll each into an egg roll wrapper. Deep-fry the 2 dumplings at 375° F until crispy. Ladle 2 ounces of chocolate syrup onto the bottom of an oval dish. Place 1 large scoop of vanilla bean ice cream at the center of the dish, then arrange the dumplings on either side. Drizzle strawberry puree over all, sprinkle with toasted coconut, and place a whole cherry at the top.

C'est Si Bon

Lagomarcino's, Moline, Illinois

Split 1 banana lengthwise and place the halves parallel on a Banana Split dish. Place 1 scoop each of vanilla and strawberry ice cream between the banana halves. Ladle 2 ounces of crushed strawberries over the vanilla ice cream, and sprinkle with chopped mixed nuts. Spoon 2 ounces of marshmallow creme over the strawberry ice cream, and sprinkle with shredded coconut. Garnish with whipped cream, sprinkle with whole salted cashews, and place a maraschino cherry at the top.

North of the Border

Behold, the most sophisticated menu of ice cream concoctions in North America. It belongs to a chainlet of ice cream parlors based, not in the good old USA, but in Toronto, Canada. If you are a restaurateur and you are reading this book, you will be particularly impressed to learn that a single individual is responsible for the creation, development, and every deliberate detail of Caffé Demetre. His name is Gary Steven Theodore, and his head office, as he explains, "consists of one person—me!" His remarkable repertoire of desserts includes two ingenious interpretations of the Banana Split, fashioned with high-concept ice cream flavors and anointed with original toppings.

Split Personality

Cut 1 banana into 1-inch chunks, and place the pieces around the edge of a Banana Split dish. Place 1 scoop each of honey-vanilla, strawberry, and chocolatta ice cream in the center of the dish. Ladle 2 ounces of five-fruit compote over the honey-vanilla, 2 ounces of sliced fresh strawberries over the strawberry, and 2 ounces of triple fudge sauce over the chocolatta ice cream. Garnish with whipped cream, sprinkle with chopped mixed nuts, and place a whole cherry at the top.

Banana Republik

Cut 1 banana into 1-inch chunks, and place the pieces around the edge of a Banana Split dish. Place 2 scoops of banana-mocha ice cream and 1 scoop of chocolatta ice cream in the center of the dish. Ladle 3 ounces of mocha fudge sauce over all. Garnish with whipped cream, sprinkle with pieces of dark chocolate, and place an inverted ice cream cone at the top.

the Banana Split is such a restorative and soothing dessert. Eating a Banana Split provides a sense of calm.

Food is memory. In a stressed-out, grown-up world, it's natural to hunger for foods that remind us of earlier, more carefree times—dodging adulthood with dishes that lift our spirits and feed our souls. In addition to our incorrigible craving for sweets, we especially enjoy foods that trigger adolescent nirvana.

Nothing brings back the memories of youth like going to a restaurant for the sole purpose of eating bananas smothered in

Mix and Match Split

Moab Diner, Moab, Utah

Split 1 banana lengthwise and place the halves parallel on a Banana Split dish. Place 3 scoops of ice cream (your choice of flavors) between the banana halves. Over the scoops of ice cream ladle 2 ounces of up to 3 toppings, with a choice of pineapple, caramel, chocolate or strawberry topping. Garnish with whipped cream, sprinkle with chopped mixed nuts if desired, and place a whole cherry at the top.

Uncle Sam Sundae

Crown Candy Kitchen, St. Louis, Missouri

Place 2 large scoops of vanilla ice cream side by side in a wide sundae bowl. Ladle 2 ounces of crushed strawberries over one scoop, and 2 ounces of crushed pineapple over the other. Slice half a banana into disks and place them around the ice cream. Garnish with whipped cream, decorate with red, white, and blue sprinkles, and place a whole cherry at the top.

Augustana Viking Special

Larson's, Rock Island, Iowa

Split 1 banana lengthwise and place the halves parallel on a Banana Split dish. Place 1 scoop each of vanilla, chocolate, and strawberry ice cream between the banana halves. Spoon 2 ounces of marshmallow creme and 2 ounces of crushed pineapple over all. Garnish with whipped cream, decorate with pretzel sticks and sugar wafers, and place 3 whole cherries at the top.

Wine & Dine

Andrew Quady is a California winemaker who specializes in delightfully idiosyncratic dessert wines, so good they're regularly served at the White House. He recommends Elysium, crafted from Black Muscat grapes, as the most appropriate accompaniment to a Banana Split. "The wine shows compatible, exotic, tropical characteristics," says Quady, who also suggests just pouring the wine over a scoop of vanilla ice cream for an Elysium Sundae.

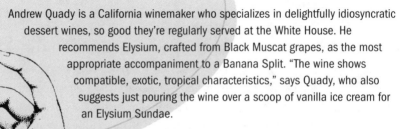

The banana evokes in our senses exotic countries, perfumed Arabia, distant islands and tropical Edens.

— Octave Uzanne

Somehow, the thought of eating a Banana Split to the tunes of Gordon Lightfoot just didn't work.

— Historian Roger Baker, on the demise of Farrell's Ice Cream Parlours

Stout-Hearted Dessert

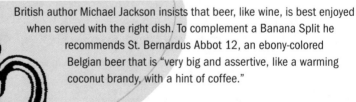

British author Michael Jackson insists that beer, like wine, is best enjoyed when served with the right dish. To complement a Banana Split he recommends St. Bernardus Abbot 12, an ebony-colored Belgian beer that is "very big and assertive, like a warming coconut brandy, with a hint of coffee."

Co-ed Sundae

Doumar's, Norfolk, Virginia

Split 1 banana lengthwise and place the halves parallel on a Banana Split dish. Place 2 scoops of vanilla ice cream between the banana halves. Ladle 3 ounces of hot fudge over all. Garnish with whipped cream, and place 2 whole cherries at the top.

Red, White, and Blue Banana Split

National Watermelon Promotion Board

Split 1 banana lengthwise and place the halves parallel on a Banana Split dish. Place 1 scoop of vanilla ice cream between the banana halves. Scoop 2 balls of watermelon, remove the seeds, and place on either side of the ice cream. Top with $\frac{1}{2}$ cup of fresh blueberries.

Caribbean Long Boat

S. Luca Confectionery, Musselburgh, Scotland

Split 1 banana lengthwise and place the halves parallel on a Banana Split dish. Place 1 scoop each of vanilla and strawberry ice cream between the banana halves. Sprinkle $\frac{1}{2}$ cup of mixed berries over the ice cream. Ladle 3 ounces of melba sauce over all. Garnish with whipped cream.

ice cream. A Banana Split may have been a reward we received as children. Now, as adults, we can indulge and treat ourselves—anytime—whether we deserve it or not. Every Banana Split comes with a side order of sentimentality.

"We live in an age like an automobile which runs a little too fast for comfort," says restaurateur George Lang, "and comfort foods are the perfect tranquilizer which makes up for the speed."

Bon Appetit magazine explains that "certain foods are inherently more comforting than others, dishes so strongly evocative of safe and happy times that the mere mention of them raises a warm and cozy glow and enhances our well-being." The Banana Split is one of those dishes from which both physical and psychic comfort truly are derived. Food historian Ruth Adams Bronz calls it "baby food for adults."

> ❝ The first thing I did when we arrived in New York City was have a Banana Split in a drug store. I'd never had one before. ❞
>
> — Adalbert Messerschmitt, German immigrant, 1948

Split the Uprights

Star quarterback of South River (New Jersey) High School, the University of Notre Dame, the Toronto Argonauts, and the Washington Redskins, Joe Theismann admits to a career-long superstition: the night before every big game, he devoured a Banana Split. "After I checked into the hotel, I had to have a Banana Split before I went to bed," says Theismann. "And if the hotel didn't serve them, I would go down to the kitchen and have a makeshift Banana Split. I was that adamant about it."

Splitting Headache

One of the quickest ways to cure a hangover is to drink a banana milkshake, sweetened with honey. Bananas calm the stomach, and, with some help from the honey, build up blood-sugar levels, while the milk soothes and rehydrates the system.

Torche de Banana Split

Kinki's, Ottawa, Ontario, Canada

*P*lace 1 slice of banana bread on an oval plate. Split 1 banana lengthwise, sprinkle the halves with sugar, heat with a small butane blowtorch or under a broiler until the sugar melts and caramelizes (see sidebar on page 58), and place them parallel on the banana bread. Place 2 scoops of ginger gelato between the banana halves. Ladle 2 ounces of chocolate syrup over one scoop and 2 ounces of caramel syrup over the other. Garnish with whipped cream.

Banana Split with a Twist

Windmill Restaurant, Dartmouth, Nova Scotia, Canada

*P*lace 1 large scoop of vanilla ice cream in the center of a hardened pastry shell (follow the directions on a store-bought pastry shell; use a bowl to shape the pastry before baking). Slice half a banana into disks, then sauté them with 4 sliced strawberries, 1 tablespoon of butter, 1 teaspoon of sugar, and a splash of Grand Marnier. Pour the fruit and liquid over the ice cream, and garnish with a swirl of whipped cream.

Almond-Crusted Banana Split

Iroquois Hotel, Mackinac Island, Michigan

*S*plit 1 banana lengthwise, dip the halves into buttermilk, roll them in crushed toasted almonds, then place them parallel on a Banana Split dish. Place 2 scoops of vanilla bean ice cream between the banana halves, and ladle 3 ounces of hot fudge over all. Garnish with whipped cream, dust with crushed malted milk balls, and place a whole cherry at the top.

BANANA DREAM

SERVICE	INGREDIENTS	PORTIONS
Footed Compote	Vanilla Ice Cream	#16 scoop, with lip
7¼" Underliner	Chocolate Ice Cream	#16 scoop, with lip
Teaspoon	Strawberry Ice Cream	#16 scoop, with lip
	Coffee Ice Cream	#16 scoop, with lip
	Banana	1 whole
	Strawberry Fruit	2 ounces
	Pineapple Fruit	1 ounce
	Chocolate Syrup	1 ounce
	Whipped Cream	2 ounces
	Chopped Nuts	1 teaspoon

1. Place four #16 scoops of ice cream in dish (1 each of vanilla, chocolate, strawberry and coffee).

2. Trim ends of banana.

3. Cut unpeeled banana in half lengthwise and then in half horizontally, for a total of four pieces.

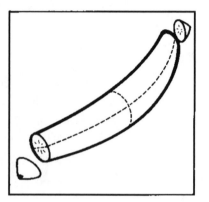

4. Place one section of peeled banana upright between each scoop of ice cream, cut surface in.

5. Ladle one ounce each of strawberry fruit over the vanilla ice cream and strawberry ice cream.

6. Ladle one ounce of pineapple fruit over the coffee ice cream.

7. Dispense one ounce of chocolate syrup over the chocolate ice cream.

8. Pile high two ounces of whipped cream in center.

9. Sprinkle one teaspoon of chopped nuts over the whipped cream.

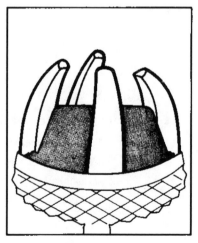

Chocolate-Dipped Banana Split

Syrah, Naples, Florida

Split 1 banana lengthwise, dip the halves into melted milk chocolate, and roll them in a mixture of coconut, crushed walnuts, and crushed pecans. Place the banana halves in a molded chocolate-chip-cookie shell (remove large baked cookie from oven and, while still hot, mold into shell by placing over a rolling pin). Place 1 scoop each of vanilla, chocolate, and strawberry ice cream between the banana halves. Slice fresh strawberries, raspberries, blackberries, cherries, and pineapple into small pieces, mix together, and spoon onto the ice cream. Drizzle caramel, chocolate, and raspberry syrups over the top, and dust with powdered sugar and unsweetened cocoa.

Banana Heaven

Blue Heaven Restaurant, Key West, Florida

Slice 1 banana lengthwise, then cut the split halves again widthwise. Place 1 tablespoon of butter, $\frac{1}{4}$ cup of brown sugar, and 2 pinches of cinnamon in a sauté pan and heat on high. When the butter is partially melted, add the banana quarters and $1\frac{1}{2}$ tablespoons of orange juice. Heat until the butter and sugar are melted and the sauce is bubbling. Add $\frac{3}{4}$ ounce of Captain Morgan Spiced Rum, and carefully ignite the rum with a long kitchen match or kitchen lighter. Pour the contents of the pan over a slice of banana bread and top with 1 large scoop of vanilla ice cream.

" Great actions are sometimes historically barren; smallest actions have taken root in the moral soil and grown like banana forests to cover whole quarters of the world. "

— Thomas Carlyle

User Friendly

In 1935, with a loan from their parents, two spunky brothers—20-year-old Priestly Blake and 18-year-old Curtis Blake—opened a modest ice cream shop in Springfield, Massachusetts. The young men named their business "Friendly," with the intention of providing neighborly service to all who visited the new enterprise. Their single menu item was a double-dip ice cream cone, which cost 5 cents.

Friendly's first Banana Split was introduced in 1940 and sold for 20 cents. At that time, the banana was placed on the bottom of the dish. Then two scoops of ice cream were placed on top of the banana, and the last scoop was placed on top of the other two. Today, the same ingredients are used, but the protocol has been updated. One scoop each of vanilla, chocolate, and strawberry ice cream is placed on a footed Banana Split dish (manufactured by Oneida Silversmiths). The vanilla ice cream is topped with chocolate sauce, the chocolate with marshmallow, and the strawberry with crushed strawberries. The scoops of ice cream are dressed with whipped cream, then dry toppings are added. The vanilla ice cream is topped with chocolate sprinkles, the chocolate with a cherry, and the strawberry with chopped peanuts. In a final gesture, the banana is sliced lengthwise and pressed against each side of the ice cream.

According to Lynn Bolton, spokesperson for Friendly's, the company holds the Banana Split in high regard. She reports that 550 company and franchised restaurants serve about 960,000 Banana Splits each year.

McSplit

McDonald's developed a one-of-a-kind restaurant at Walt Disney World in Orlando, Florida, named Mickey D's, where you can work up your own Banana Split by selecting three scoops of ice cream and either hot fudge or butterscotch sauce. Mickey D's adds the banana, tops it with walnuts in syrup, then caps it with loads of whipped cream and cherries. It's called the Top Banana.

Banana Split Waffles

Magnolia Manor Bed & Breakfast, Thibodaux, Louisiana

$\frac{1}{4}$ cup butter or margarine, melted

$\frac{1}{4}$ to $\frac{1}{2}$ cup sugar

1 teaspoon vanilla extract

2 cups milk

2 large (or 3 medium) eggs, separated

2 cups self-rising flour

2 bananas, mashed

$\frac{3}{4}$ cup chopped mixed nuts

Sliced strawberries, for garnish

Whipped cream, for garnish

Chopped pecans, for garnish

❶ Put the butter and sugar in a mixing bowl and stir until the sugar dissolves. Stir in the vanilla. Add the milk a little at a time, stirring continuously.

❷ In a small bowl, beat the egg yolks, then add them to the butter mixture.

❸ Add the flour, a little at a time, until the mixture thickens slightly and will pour slowly. (You may use a little more or a little less than 2 cups.)

❹ Add the mashed bananas to the mixture.

❺ Whip the egg whites until stiff, then fold them gently into the mixture.

❻ Stir in the chopped nuts.

❼ Pour 1 tablespoon of batter into each compartment of a hot waffle iron and cover the iron. Bake according to manufacturer's directions. Repeat with remaining batter.

❽ Top waffles with fresh sliced strawberries, whipped cream, and chopped pecans. Serve with melted butter and syrup.

> **Time flies like an arrow; fruit flies like a banana.**
>
> — Groucho Marx

XCugat

America's fascination with any conglomeration containing bananas and ice cream is simultaneously innocent and unabashedly senti-mental. The Banana Split represents a culinary anchor in a world of uncertainty, and it summons appreciation for the permanence of a classic and the notion that truly good things will not fade away.

What may be lost or forgotten, however, is that the Banana Split paved the way for post-Victorian culinary liberation early in the 20th century. It was one of the earliest building blocks for what is now called American cuisine. Today, restaurateurs

The Last Straw

"It's the only Banana Split you can sip through a straw," reads the menu at Ellen's Stardust Diner on Broadway in midtown Manhattan. The Elvis-era retro-diner, owned by Ellen Hart Sturm, a former New York City "Miss Subway," features singing waiters who deliver soda fountain fare, including killer milkshakes, to the theater crowd. The Lickety-Split has all the ingredients of a classic Banana Split, except they're *all shook up*.

Banana Split Cake

SERVES 6 TO 8

Bistro 420, Winston-Salem, North Carolina

For the layer cake:

2 cups all-purpose flour

1½ cups sugar

1½ teaspoons baking powder

¾ teaspoon baking soda

½ teaspoon salt

1 cup mashed ripe banana
(3 medium bananas)

½ cup buttermilk

½ cup shortening

2 eggs

1 teaspoon vanilla extract

For the filling and frosting:

2 cups sweetened whipped cream or 6 ounces
Cool Whip

1 cup sliced fresh strawberries

1 8¼-ounce can crushed pineapple,
well drained

10 ounces chocolate syrup

½ cup chopped peanuts

Whipped cream, for garnish

1 whole cherry

Sliced strawberries, for garnish

1 banana, sliced into disks, for garnish

❶ Preheat the oven to 350° F. Grease and flour two 9-inch round baking pans.

❷ In a large mixing bowl, combine the flour, sugar, baking powder, baking soda, and salt. Add the mashed banana, buttermilk, shortening, eggs, and vanilla. Beat with an electric mixer on low speed till combined. Beat on medium speed for 3 minutes. Pour batter into pans.

❸ Bake for 30 minutes or until a toothpick inserted into the center of the cake comes out clean. Cool on wire racks for 10 minutes, then remove cakes from pans and cool completely on wire racks.

❺ Divide the whipped cream into equal halves. Fold the strawberries into one half and the pineapple into the other half.

❻ Place the bottom cake layer on a serving plate. Spread it with the strawberry cream, all the way to the edges. Drizzle chocolate syrup over this, then top with the second cake layer.

❼ Cover the top layer with the pineapple cream, and drizzle with chocolate syrup.

❽ Sprinkle with peanuts, add a dollop of plain whipped cream, and place a whole cherry at the top. Garnish with sliced strawberries and banana disks.

The Original Comfort Food

Banana Split Sandwich

The Banana Split is a nearly perfect dessert, but, unfortunately, not very portable. So concluded a student at Swarthmore College near Philadelphia, who, according to the college newspaper, solved the problem with an inspired formula:

Peel 1 banana and place it on a clean plate. Mash it with a fork and use a knife to spread the resulting banana "butter" on a waffle. Place 1 scoop of ice cream on top, and spread it firmly over the banana. Finally, drizzle chocolate syrup over the ice cream, and cover the "sandwich" with another waffle.

Key Words

Brain freeze. When very cold food or drink touches the center of the palate (roof of the mouth), the temperature can affect nerves that control blood flow to the head. If you eat your Banana Split too fast, the ice cream may cause your head to pound and hurt, as blood vessels swell up. Try warming each bite just a bit in the front of your mouth before swallowing.

Split Loyalties

Cole Porter's 1938 Broadway musical, *Leave It to Me,* was a satire on the Soviet Union in which the American ambassador is homesick for Topeka, Kansas, and continually longs for a "Double Banana Split."

lure sweet-toothed customers into capping off their meals with the comfort of that classic Split, updated with new flavors and twists; there are as many versions as there are theories on what should go into it. In a world where it seems as if popularity has become the one true measure of significance, the Banana Split appears on menus in practically every large city on the planet. No matter how you slice it, the Banana Split is here to stay.

To view the Banana Split in the wider context of derivative dishes is to appreciate even more fully its ageless allure. If it is going to be properly commemorated, it should be as familiar as possible. This small glimpse of the many directions it has taken, even while remaining informed by tradition, is an appropriate salute to David Strickler's magnum opus of a dessert.

A Banana a Day . . .

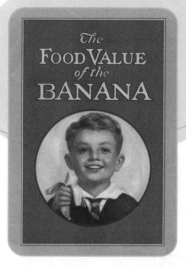

The FOOD VALUE of the BANANA

Compared to an apple, a single banana has 50 percent more food energy, four times the protein, almost three times the phosphorus, five times the Vitamin A and iron, and at least twice the amount of other vitamins and minerals.

Bites of Passage

David Lebovitz, author of *Ripe for Dessert* and *The Great Book of Chocolate,* writes about his earliest memories of Banana Splits in a then-rural part of Connecticut.

> What always upset me was that they used vanilla ice cream to make Sundaes and Banana Splits just about everywhere. Sorry, but I wanted chocolate—chocolate sauce, bananas, marshmallow (better than whipped cream), all covering three generous scoops of chocolate ice cream. Chocolate ice cream is for the hard-core dessert people, vanilla is for those who can't handle so much excess.
>
> And in those days, for an extra 5 cents, you could get a cup, served on the side, of warm buttered walnuts to scatter over the whole thing.
>
> So now that I'm an adult, how do I make a perfect Banana Split? Three scoops of homemade bittersweet chocolate ice cream with big chunks of dark chocolate within, a generous ladleful of marshmallow, a red banana that's been caramelized in butter, and a bowlful on the side of a mixture of warm buttered nuts, cashews, hazelnuts, walnuts, and macadamia nuts with just a few grains of salt tossed in.

Best Banana Split Names:

Three Stooges Banana Split (PJ's Ice Cream Parlor, Farmington, Pennsylvania)
Yellow Submarine (Chubby's, Lehi, Utah)
Teeny Bikini Banana Split (Miramonte, St. Helena, California)
Oceanbound Banana Yacht (Ice Cream Castle, Ocean City, Maryland)
Banana Dream Boat (Average Joe's, North Bay, Ontario, Canada)
Bing-Bong-Bang-Bambididly-Boom-Banana Split (Moosehead Canadian Bar, Moscow, Russia)
Nirvana Banana Split (Carson Street Café at the Golden Nugget Casino, Las Vegas, Nevada)
Yummy Nanner Split (Fellini Restaurant, Portland, Oregon)
Bigfoot Banana Split (Pancake Train, Hobart, Tasmania)
Bay of Pigs (Asia de Cuba, New York, New York, and Los Angeles, California)
Caramel Miranda (Avalon Restaurant, Lahaina, Maui, Hawaii)
Bigger Than Bill (Mullen's Dairy Bar, Watertown, Wisconsin)

Split Decision

The foreign media poked fun at America's 2000 presidential election debacle between George W. Bush and Al Gore. Not so subtly suggesting that the contest resembled the election process in a banana republic, the headline in the *Times of India* jeered, "American Banana Split."

You Are What You Eat

Executive Pastry Chef James Foran of the Westgate Hotel's Le Fountainebleau in San Diego, California, created a "light" Banana Split for, as he calls it, "the California lifestyle." First, a baby banana is split, caramelized, and placed on a 3½ x ½-inch round of angel food cake. The banana halves cradle scoops of vanilla bean, chocolate mocha, and strawberry sorbet (the vanilla bean sorbet is made with a nonfat milk base and the chocolate mocha sorbet is made with cocoa powder, fresh espresso, and nonfat milk as well). The dessert is garnished with roasted meringue, sprinkled with dried banana chips and pieces of pistachio praline (made without butter), then topped with a fresh Bing cherry. Tableside accompaniments include warm cocoa sauce made with low-fat buttermilk, caramel passion fruit sauce, strawberry lime chutney, and a Bing cherry port sauce.

banana contains the equivalent of 5 level teaspoons of sugar.

NATURE SEALS BANANAS IN A GERM-PROOF PACKAGE

ENJOY YOUR FAVORITE CEREAL WITH SWEET, RIPE BANANAS

COOKING GIVES BANANAS A DIFFERENT, DELICIOUS FLAVOR

ALL MEASUREMENTS USED IN THESE RECIPES ARE LEVE

BANANAS ARE AVAILABLE ALL YEAR 'ROUND

FOR SWEETEST FLAVOR... A BANANA FLECKED WITH BROWN

MEASUREMENTS (Approximate)

This information is based upon the use of standard level measurements and one average-sized banana.

1 AVERAGE-SIZED BANANA (100 to 120 calories)

Sliced or diced = 1 cup, 30 slices (⅛ inch thick)
Mashed or whipped = ½ cup

1 CUP OF BANANAS

Sliced or diced = 1 banana
Mashed or whipped = 2 bananas

1 POUND OF BANANAS

Unpeeled = 3 to 4 bananas
Peeled = 4 to 5 bananas
Sliced or diced = 4 to 5 bananas (4 cups)
Mashed or whipped = 4 to 5 bananas (2 cups)

PRINTED IN U. S. A., 1950

ONE AVERAGE-SIZED BANANA

VITAMINS per 100 grams

A	250-335 International Units
B₁ (Thiamine)	42-54 Micrograms
B₂ or G (Riboflavin)	88 Micrograms
Niacin (Nicotinic Acid)	.6 Milligrams
C (Ascorbic Acid)	10-11 Milligrams

MINERALS milligrams per 100 grams

Sodium 42.0	Manganese .6	Sulfur 12.0
Potassium 373.0	Copper .2	Chlorine 125.0
Calcium 8.0	Iron .6	Iodine .003
Magnesium 31.0	Phosphorus 28.0	

Home Economics Department

UNITED FRUIT COMPANY

PIER 3, NORTH RIVER, NEW YORK 6, N.Y.

Banana Split in Paradise

Maui, Hawaii, is an enchanting Pacific isle of rain forests, valleys, springs, slopes, waterfalls, sandy beaches, exotic flowers, and every indigenous tropical ingredient one needs to make a truly native Banana Split. Even the bananas are homegrown. Local Hawaiian "apple bananas" are more flavorful than supermarket bananas, with a unique apple aftertaste.

At the Maui Tropical Plantation, just off Honoapi'ilani Highway in central Maui, you can take a tram tour through the fields of a working plantation, then stop by the restaurant to experience what a Banana Split can achieve when you send it to Hawaii for a vacation.

Plantation Banana Split

Split 1 plantation-grown native Hawaiian banana lengthwise and place the halves parallel on a Banana Split dish. Place 3 scoops of Tahitian vanilla ice cream between the banana halves. Ladle 2 ounces of puree of Waimea strawberries over the first scoop, 2 ounces of crushed Maui Gold pineapple over the second, and 2 ounces of bittersweet Hawaiian chocolate–sugar cane syrup over the third. Garnish with whipped cream, and sprinkle with freshly picked macadamia nuts.

> **He is an anachronism, rooted in an age when a date wasn't a disco, then your place or mine, but rather a double feature at the local Rialto, then maybe a Banana Split at the corner soda fountain.**
>
> — Novelist Mordecai Richler on Wayne Gretzky

Leave Nothing to Chance

Everyone who worked at Howard Johnson's restaurants adhered to "the Bible," a set of standards for cleanliness, service, recipes, and menu items, developed and rigidly enforced by the tireless Howard Johnson himself. He would allow no variation from one restaurant to another. The Bible stipulated that there be 19 to 21 clams per portion; that every hot dog was to be sliced exactly six times along its side; that coffee was to be poured to just three-eighths of an inch from the top of the cup. As for Howard Johnson's Banana Splits, he required careful attention to their consistently attractive presentation, and he provided a diagram for servers to follow exactly.

> **❝ Stephen King is so popular that if he'd printed a book on a banana, half a million people would have shown up to get their banana. ❞**
>
> **— Jeff Bezos, founder and CEO of online bookseller Amazon.com**

Sweet Home Chicago

Margie's has stood like a rock in Chicago's Bucktown neighborhood since George Poulos opened the sweet shop for business in 1921. And, to judge by Margie's, great big Banana Splits will never be in danger of becoming extinct. Every day gleeful customers squeeze into the shop and line up elbow to elbow to choose from sundaes, sodas, candies, and 12 different Banana Splits—including the Royal George, with 22 scoops of ice cream, 7 toppings, and half a dozen bananas sliced into disks.

According to Margie's third-generation owner, Peter Poulos, a true "Banana Split" is served with banana halves at the bottom; a "Banana Boat," with banana halves at the sides; and a "Banana Royale," with bananas cut into slices so that each spoonful holds a bite of both banana and ice cream.

Royal Treatment

Dairy Queen stores nationwide
sell more than 25 million Banana Splits each year, according to Ed Watson, chief operating officer of the American Dairy Queen Corporation. Among Dairy Queen's "Royal Treats," the chain's menu of top-of-the-line sundaes, "we don't have any that outperform the Banana Split," says Watson.

> **I love the Banana Split. It cures depression and is better than drinking.**
>
> **— Chris Isaak**

A Greater Glory

The Knickerbocker Glory is a very British ice cream confection, heaped into a tall glass. To assemble a classic version, place 2 ounces of crushed strawberries in the bottom of a tall sundae goblet, then add 1 large scoop of vanilla ice cream. Cover with 2 ounces of marshmallow syrup, and sprinkle with chopped hazelnuts. Add 2 ounces of crushed peaches, followed by 1 large scoop of strawberry ice cream. Garnish with whipped cream, sprinkle with chopped pistachios, and place (as a Brit might say) a green-coloured cherry surmounting the whole!

At Cozies at Gorleston-on-Sea in Norfolk, the Knickerbocker Glory formula is put to good use when a Banana Split is made, with instructions "as above, but laid down with banana."

Credits

The following illustrations appear courtesy of sources as noted. Credits are given in the order in which illustrations appear in the text.

Front Matter P. ix, Chiquita Brands International.

Chapter 1 P. 2, vintage postcard. P. 4 (top), Chiquita Brands International. P. 5 (bottom), Library of Congress. P. 6 (top), vintage postcard; (bottom), © 2003-2004 www.clipart.com. P. 7, vintage postcard. P. 8 (bottom), Chiquita Brands International. P. 9, vintage postcard. P. 10 (bottom), Chiquita Brands International. P. 11, vintage postcards. P. 12 (bottom), © 2003-2004 www.clipart.com. P. 13, Chiquita Brands International.

Chapter 2 P. 14, Chiquita Brands International. P. 22, Strickler family. P. 26, *The Ice Cream Review* (October, 1939). P. 27 (bottom), Latrobe [Pennsylvania] Historical Society. P. 29, Saint Vincent College. P. 31, Chiquita Brands International.

Chapter 3 P. 32, Fruit Dispatch Company booklet (1940). P. 33, Hazard family. P. 34, Wilmington [Ohio] Historical Society. P. 38 (bottom), Michael Turback. P. 40, Library of Congress. P. 46, Juliet Turback.

Chapter 4 P. 50, Chiquita Brands International. Pp. 51, 52, 54 (top), 56, and 58, Movie Star News. Pp. 60, 64, 68, 70, 72, and 73 (top), Chiquita Brands International.

Chapter 5 P. 76, Chiquita Brands International. P. 80, Franchise Associates, South Weymouth, Massachusetts. P. 96, Jaxson's Ice Cream Parlor, Dania Beach, Florida.

Chapter 6 P. 100 (top), International Banana Club; (bottom), Movie Star News. P. 116, Chiquita Brands International.

Chapter 7 Pp. 120, 121, and 132, Norman's, Coral Gables, Florida.

Chapter 8 P. 138, Chiquita Brands International. P. 148, Franchise Associates, South Weymouth, Massachusetts. P. 150 (top), Library of Congress. P. 154, Juliet Turback. Pp. 155 and 157 (bottom), Chiquita Brands International.

Other images © 2003-2004 www.clipart.com.

Recipes

Where To Eat Banana Splits

Index